W9-BYY-266

By Jenny Rosenstrach

Dinner: The Playbook

Dinner: A Love Story

DINNER

the playbook

DINNER
the playbook

**A 30-DAY PLAN FOR MASTERING
THE ART OF THE FAMILY MEAL**

Jenny Rosenstrach

BALLANTINE BOOKS
TRADE PAPERBACKS
NEW YORK

A Ballantine Books Trade Paperback Original

Copyright © 2014 by Jenny Rosenstrach

All rights reserved.

Published in the United States by Ballantine Books, an imprint of
Random House, a division of Random House LLC,
a Penguin Random House Company, New York.

BALLANTINE and the HOUSE colophon are registered trademarks
of Random House LLC.

Library of Congress Cataloging-in-Publication Data

Rosenstrach, Jenny.
Dinner: The Playbook:
a 30-day plan for mastering the art of the family meal/Jenny Rosenstrach.
pages   cm
Includes index.
ISBN 978-0-345-54980-8
eBook ISBN 978-0-345-54981-5
1. Cooking.   2. Dinners and dining.   3. Families.   I. Title.
TX714.R6735 2014
642—dc23 2013033023

Printed in the United States of America on acid-free paper

www.ballantinebooks.com

24689753

Design by Kristina DiMatteo

For
Dinner: A Love Story
blog readers . . .
and stressed-out parents everywhere.
You are my people!

CONTENTS

— x —

INTRODUCTION

— 5 —

THE RULES

— 21 —

HOW TO GET STARTED

— 55 —

GO-TO WEEKNIGHT MEALS

— 153 —

22 QUICK SIDES

— 165 —

KEEP-THE-SPARK-ALIVE DINNERS

— 201 —

WORKBOOK

— 208 —

ACKNOWLEDGMENTS

— 210 —

INDEX

INTRODUCTION

A few years ago, I started a blog called Dinner: A Love Story. I started it because, well, because I had lost my job and I needed something to do with myself. But I also started it because I felt like dinner—specifically *family* dinner—was getting a bad rap. Instead of being a ritual to look forward to, a gathering place where everyone could swap stories and reconnect with each other after a jam-packed day, eating dinner together had become a (source of stress) for a lot of us, a thousand-piece puzzle that couldn't be solved. Even though most parents *want* to make it happen regularly, and even though most parents *know* how many good things can come from sitting down with their kids at the end of the day, it's just too hard to organize a homemade meal, too overwhelming to figure out what to cook, too impossible to coordinate schedules, too frustrating to feed picky eaters. And, hey, why bother when it's so easy to just crank the oven to 400°F and heat up any one of the pizzas, tacos, or boxes of chicken nuggets in the freezer?

I called my blog "a love story" ♥ because—with the exception of a few harrowing years when my two daughters were toddlers—family dinner has, for the most part, been a romance, a haven, a magnetic north, the direction I am headed every day, no matter what chaos is going on outside the four walls of my kitchen. I was lucky enough to work as a food editor in magazines for many years, so I'd amassed a pretty solid archive of family-friendly recipes and organizing strategies. I launched the blog with the idea that I could take all that I had learned and help people turn dinner into their own love story. I went live on March 18, 2010, with a post called "Weaning Them Off the Nugget."

Four years, one book, and millions of readers later, I've written nearly nine hundred posts covering family dinner from every angle imaginable: from easy recipes to pep talks to shopping tutorials to entertaining with kids to vacation dinners to holiday dinners to convincing the kids to talk at the table to cookbook reviews ✔ to kitchen gear recommendations to *stories*—hundreds and hundreds of stories about how a real family makes it work every day. I even make a point to periodically show images of family dinner in popular culture—from *The Incredibles* to *Annie Hall* to *Fantastic Mr. Fox*. You might say I've drilled deep on the topic.

In spite of this, what question do you think I get asked most by my readers?

It isn't "What should I make tonight?" or "What is your favorite dinner?" or "You sure this is the best use of a college degree?"

It's this: *Where do I start?*

And after four years, I finally have an answer: You start with a calendar, a strategy, a well-considered batch of simple recipes, and a monthlong commitment to making dinner happen.

That's where I started: With **30 days and 30 dinners.** Simple dinners—like the ones in this book. A decade later, though work and extracurriculars threaten to destabilize our busy, fragile atom of a household every day of the week, we're still sitting down together every night and, unless I'm in major denial, still reaping the rewards.

Here's how we got there.

The Great Dinner Rut of 2006

Long before I launched the blog, and even before I started keeping my Dinner Diary (in which I've **recorded every meal** I've cooked since February 22, 1998. For real!), sitting down to a meal together had always played a disproportionately large role in my relationship with my husband, **A**ndy. It had started during our courtship in college, when we'd celebrate finishing a paper on early Pequot Indian poetry by treating ourselves to a dinner out at the fancy Italian place—the place that introduced us to a strange cheese called Gorgonzola (what's up, early '90s?) and served a tiramisù that was about as delicate as a four-by-four. Dinner remained the bright spot of our day when we first got married and had entire weekends to devote to expanding our recipe repertoires, subwaying it all over Brooklyn, where we lived at the time, and the outer boroughs of New York City hunting down tamarind concentrate for some *New York Times* recipe that we really had no business attempting, given our limited culinary chops. Dinner was especially sacred for us when our two babies were babies and we'd sink into our kitchen chairs after their bedtime to a ritual that was simple, delicious, and kind of magical in its replenishing power. We'd sit down, just the two of us, and have our first conversation of the day that wasn't about Pablo the Backyardigan, then clean up the table without Dustbustering the Cheerios under the hulking, space-eating high chair. Until that point in my life, I never knew how much my identity as a grown-up was wrapped up in a homemade spinach omelet and a glass of Chardonnay.

But as our daughters grew their way through the toddler phase seemingly in unison (they are only twenty months apart), we started to feel like our **adult-only dinners** after the kids went to bed were a form of cheating. We had both been raised in families where **dinnertime** was a command performance, where everyone sat down together. Why weren't we at least trying to do the same thing? Maybe, we thought over a quick Bolognese one night, *maybe* we should try folding our actual *family* into family dinner?

This didn't go quite as smoothly as we had hoped.

There was the time ⓒ issue. Or, perhaps more accurately phrased: the *lack-of-time* issue. We were both working full-time and not usually walking in the door until six thirty or seven, at which point it felt like someone might have announced over a loudspeaker: *"And they're off!"* With the girls' eight-thirty bedtime (and bath time and story time and please-just-one-*more*-story time) looming over us, we heard the ticking of a stopwatch (or was it a time bomb?) throughout the entire evening. We hardly ever considered a recipe **unless it had the word *quick* in the title,** and it turned out that was an accurate way to describe not just the making of dinner but the consumption of it. Our family meals when the girls were three and four years old lasted, on average, two minutes and thirteen seconds. Catching up on the day's events? Savoring the Chicken Parmesan? Having a *conversation*? That **part of the ritual** seemed to be for other families in other universes.

I'd say the biggest dinner obstacle we faced, though, was something we identified early on as *ingestus particulare*, a condition more commonly known as (*picky eating.*) Abby, our then-three-year-old, had only a few meals that one might slot in the "surefire" category: **plain** pasta, **plain** rice, **plain** breaded chicken cutlets. Naturally, two of Abby's "surefires" perfectly overlapped with her four-year-old sister Phoebe's "nonstarters." This was terribly frustrating for two tired parents who were just trying to make one meal that **everyone would eat.** We were so psyched that Phoebe was somehow born to love any kind of seafood—oysters, clams, salmon, smoked trout, once even shark. (We spent a lot of those years knocking on wood.) But where family dinner was concerned, this impressive feat meant nothing, given that her sister would pretend to like flounder for a bite or two, before realizing how much more fun it would be to see what flounder looked like when it was chewed up and spat out on her plate.

In other words, even though we had built a pretty solid archive of dinners during our years as (childless) kitchen enthusiasts, it suddenly seemed that all those years had been for naught. Where we'd once approach dinner by asking, "What are we in the mood for tonight?" **?** (or, even more luxuriously, "What is good at the market today?"), now it was, "What can we make for the girls tonight that won't ignite a revolt?" We started calling this small pool of dinners our Lowest Common Denominator Meals. And they tasted every bit as exciting as they sound. If you took one look at my dinner diary during that long stretch in 2006, you would notice a lot of one-word meal descriptions:

Cutlets, BURGERS, *Pizza*

Then the week following:
Cutlets, BURGERS, *Pizza*

Then: .... BURGERS, **Cutlets, Cutlets**
Then: .... *Pizza, Pizza,* BURGERS
Then: .... BURGERS, BURGERS, **Cutlets**

We had fallen into what we came to call the Great Dinner Rut of 2006. And one day, I just decided, *to hell with it*. If cooking was ever going to be rewarding again, if the kids were going to develop a sense of adventure around food and learn to try new things, if we held out any hope of establishing a **family dinner ritual** that resembled the ones we had grown up with, well, then, I needed to do something. ✗ I needed to break out of the rut. Like *immediately*. I mean, how many bone-dry turkey burgers can a woman be expected to eat in the course of two weeks?

So on January 14, 2007, we launched Operation 30 Days, 30 Dinners. Thirty brand-new dinners in thirty days.

I have no idea how I came up with this idea. I suppose I recognized on some level that the rut was so deep that I needed to do something drastic and goal-oriented. And for whatever reason, it felt like an all-or-nothing proposition: If I wanted the girls to be on board with me, I had to fully inhabit the mission and turn it into a Capital-**E** Event. This is the way it would work: Andy and I would cook a new dinner every single night for a month—brand-new to me and Andy, and brand-new to the girls. **New dishes, new ingredients, new colors, new textures and techniques.** All those recipes collecting dust in the Someday-We'll-Make-This File? All those fabulous restaurant meals we'd eat, then say, "I wish the girls would let us make this at home"? All those cookbook pages that had been dog-eared by some pre-kid-era imposter . . . me!? Now was the time to try those recipes. Now was the time to *take back dinner*.

I did not expect thirty days of sunshine and rainbows. I did not enter into this (OK, somewhat insane) challenge thinking it was going to be easy or even necessarily effective. I certainly had no delusions that it would forever change the landscape of our dinner table.

But, amazingly, it sort of . . . *did*.

Don't get me wrong here. I do not mean to suggest that every meal garnered an A+ from every diner every night. Nor do I mean to suggest that we were walking through the door and whipping up Mario Batali's beef-cheek ravioli on a Tuesday and Thomas Keller's pan-fried trout on a Wednesday. Remember, **we are talking about** *kids*. Kids and *eating*, no less. Which means that success is always going to be relative. If you asked me how many meals from the original thirty we still make today, six years later (see page 3 for the full lineup), I'd estimate it at (six or seven keepers,) depending on which way the wind is blowing on soup. (Some days they look at me like I'm Cruella De Vil when I serve it, and some days they pick up their bowls and lick them cleaner than Iris, our Boston terrier, ever could.)

But in the end, adding new recipes to the repertoire was almost beside the point. As I wrote about in my first book, *Dinner: A Love Story,* the result of our experiment ended up being something I had never expected: Over the course of those intense thirty days—working full-time, have I mentioned that?—we gave our tired repertoire a much-needed shot of inspiration, we exposed our daughters to new things, and, most important, we started the long process of locating, then flexing, then building up their adventure muscles. Which is a long way of saying that it became normal for our kids to **Try New Things**. And when we had kids who approached the table with that mindset, we found ourselves in a whole new world.

How is this even possible? you ask. *And are you sure you have not been sniffing some of that white pepper you occasionally sneak onto the kids' chicken?*

I am here to tell you that **healthy, wholesome, sane, enjoyable,**

and enjoyably messy family dinners *are* possible. And this book is going to help you get there.

Remember Abby, from a few pages ago, who was famous for taking one reluctant bite of flounder, chewing it for about eight minutes, then horking it up on her plate? She's now **10** years old, and last week, she did the honors of placing the family order at our local Japanese restaurant. (Our favorite way to celebrate a week of home-cooked dinners? A Friday night out.) These words actually came out of her once fish-hating (but really, really sweet, I swear) little mouth: "Two orders shrimp siu mai, one order salmon teriyaki, one yellowtail scallion roll, six pieces salmon sushi, one piece red snapper, and one spicy shrimp tempura roll." And then, for good measure, **"Does that come with miso soup?"**

(Yes, I just turned into the mother who brags about her kid eating sushi. To preempt any eye-rolling, I'd like to remind you that my other daughter, Phoebe, *doesn't like pasta*. Pasta, the easiest, cheapest, most conventionally kid-friendly food on earth. And neither of my girls likes eggs. I'd trade sushi for those two aces in the hole *any day*.)

Are there things Abby still doesn't eat? Yes. Is it possible that the sheer act of growing up helped her along with her fish issue as much as any thirty-day parent-inflicted dinnertime torture did? Of course. Some aversions might not ever go away. (See: eggs.) This is not a book that's going to solve your every picky-eater need, nor will it cure once and for all the Sibling Shouting Syndrome infecting small diners across the country.

But if you follow the instructions laid out for you and stick to the plan, I can pretty much (guarantee) that you will start thinking about dinner differently and that, as a happy result, your kids probably will, too.

Like, for instance, instead of thinking about dinner as one more task to ✔ check off your endless to-do list, you will start thinking of it as your *reward* for checking the tasks off your endless to-do list. Instead of thinking of it as a source of anxiety, you will think of it as a form of therapy, as the time of day when you finally get a breather. And instead of resenting the relentlessness of it—*My God, is it here again? Didn't I just make a whole stinking pot of meatballs yesterday?*—you might even come to cherish dinner's role as your family's North Star. And also, you and your children will eat incredibly well. **I promise.**

READY?

DINNER
the playbook

MY 30 DINNERS

*Before we begin, I thought you'd like to see
the final lineup of dinners that Andy and I made for our
30-day challenge (including their report card grades)
back in 2007. More than twenty were successfully
consumed, and about a half dozen are still in heavy
rotation today (and oh, what a delicious half dozen they
are!), but maybe you'll have better luck with the other
twenty-four in your house. If I've learned
anything in my years writing about family dinners,
it's that one parent's failure is another
parent's victory. The most I can do is give you options,
strategies, and someone to blame (me!)
if it all goes south.*

DAY 1:
Peanut Butter
Noodles
(Sesame Noodles)**
Grade: B+

DAY 2:
Spaghetti Omelet*
Grade: B

DAY 3:
Salmon in Braised
Tomatoes
Grade: B+

DAY 4:
Braised Beef
Short Ribs**
(or Slow-Cooker
Korean Short Ribs,
page 120)
Grade: A

DAY 5:
Lamb Burgers
with Chutney
Potatoes*
Grade: A-

DAY 6:
Orecchiette with
Sausage and
Broccoli**
Grade: A-

DAY 7:
Tortilla Soup*
Grade: B-

DAY 8:
Prosciutto,
Cheddar, and
Apple Sandwich
Grade: A-

DAY 9:
Shrimp (or Fish)
Tacos on
Homemade
Tortillas*
Grade: A+

DAY 10:
Chicken with
Bacony Brussels
Sprouts**
Grade: A

DAY 11:
Shrimp Curry
Grade: A-

DAY 12:
Steak Salad
with Horseradish
Dressing*
Grade: B

DAY 13:
Salmon with
Peas and Mint
Grade: B+

DAY 14:
Swedish
Meatballs**
Grade: B+

DAY 15:
Tomato White
Bean Soup with
Shrimp**
Grade: B+

DAY 16:
Mustard Pork
Chops with
Gnocchi
Grade: B+

DAY 17:
Pasta with Arugula,
Pine Nuts, and
Parmesan
Grade: B+

DAY 18:
Market Salad
with Green
Goddess Dressing
Grade: B

DAY 19:
Trout with Beans
and Almonds*
Grade: A

DAY 20:
Cranberry-Glazed
Pork Tenderloin
Grade: B

DAY 21:
Pan-Fried Whole
Wheat Pizzas
(page 84)
Grade: A-

DAY 22:
Cioppino
(aka Tomato
Fish Stew)
(page 128)
Grade: A

DAY 23:
Veal Scallopini
with Garlicky
Spinach
Grade: B/B+

DAY 24:
Vietnamese
Lettuce Wraps*
Grade: B+

DAY 25:
Chicken Stew
with Biscuits*
Grade: B+

DAY 26:
Roasted Salmon
with Lentils
(page 136)
Grade: B+

DAY 27:
Grilled Chicken
with Peanut Curry
Sauce (page 96)
Grade: B/B+

DAY 28:
Lamb Chops,
Broiled Tomato,
and Couscous
Grade: A-

DAY 29:
Sweet-Potato
Lasagna
Grade: B-

DAY 30:
Citrusy Soy
Swordfish with
Soba Noodles
Grade: A-

*All grades
administered by
me, based on a
combination of
factors: how easy
the meal was to
prepare, how
many people at
the table liked it,
and how brutal
the cleanup was.*

* You can find the recipe on my blog, dinneralovestory.com.
** You can find the recipe in my first book, Dinner: A Love Story.

THE RULES

A FEW THINGS TO KEEP IN MIND BEFORE YOU BEGIN

RULE 1: *Don't Wait for the Stars to Align*

Once you decide to sign on to the plan, I know that the first thing you're going to do is check your calendar. Because you are a parent, and parents don't make a move without first consulting the master schedule. You want to make sure there's no travel soccer tournament that month, no nail-biting audition of *Finian's Rainbow* to prepare your daughter for, no presentation for work that you're going to be obsessing over, no activities that are going to disrupt and distract from all the planning and cooking. I understand this impulse completely—believe me, I do—but I strongly recommend that you resist the temptation and just decide right here and now to begin on Sunday. I don't have any idea if that means tomorrow or six days from when you are reading this, but either way, if you have a few hours on a Sunday, you can get yourself in good shape to kick-start the program.

Now, obviously, if Sunday is the day you are scheduled for the twins' C-section, Sunday is probably not a good idea. But if you are sitting down and looking for "a month that works," I want to save you some time and just tell you now that you are not going to find one. And besides, what are you looking for exactly? A month with no plans? A month with no school? No camp? No work? No sports? No pottery, karate, chess, play rehearsal? No tap dancing? No book report due tomorrow even though the kid, God love him, had three freaking weeks to write it? No teething? No witching hours? No train running late? No meltdown over who gets the green one and who gets the red one? No car-pool coordinating that would make an air traffic controller look lazy? No recitals, games, play-dates, meetings, parent observation days at ballet that sounded so sweet and precious until the day you have to figure out how to hang up on your client in order to get there?

I'm sorry if this sounds harsh, but you're not going to find it. And even if you did, that's not the kind of month you want anyway. Because what exactly are you proving if you cook every night for thirty days with no pressure and no stress? What are you learning? It would be like preparing for a white-water-rafting trip by lounging on an inner tube in the town pool. The idea here is to work within the swirl of your messy, beautiful chaos. To *embrace* it. So no excuses. Circle this Sunday as Day 1.

RULE 2: *Enlist the Whole Family*

I can't emphasize this enough: If you've spent any time on my blog or read my first book, you know that a crucial part of what keeps the dinner engine running in our house is the fact that both my husband and I know how to cook. Because I am the one with the more flexible schedule during the week, most of the time I'm the one getting dinner together from Monday through Friday. But on nights when I'm overextended or have a late meeting or just can't bring myself to do it, I know Andy will step in and make his Pan-Roasted Chicken Thighs with Potato-Carrot Hash (twenty minutes; page 68) or a quick Roasted Salmon and Asparagus with Spicy Mayo and Chives (twenty minutes; page 66). This is important not only for the short view (*yum, delicious, seconds, please!*) but for the *long* view, because psychologically, it helps to know that *it's not all on me*. When you share the load, dinner is a group effort, a family project. If it's all on you, it's just a burden.

Now, what if it's only you? Or what if your partner or spouse doesn't know how to cook?

Here is what you do: You call *bullsh*t* on your partner. *ANYONE CAN COOK.*

Because here's the thing: We're not going for Michelin stars. We're talking about preparing food for your own dinner table, the one where your

In Case You Are Flipping Through This Book and Saying to Yourself, "Suckers! Who's Going to Buy This Gimmicky Self-Help Book?"

In response to this, I'd like to point out that in your young life, you've probably attempted all sorts of crazy diet plans. (Or, in my case, at least *entertained* attempting all sorts of crazy diet plans.) You probably ate Snackwells by the dozen when "fat-free" foods were all the rage in the 1990s. I'm sure there were a few bunless burger nights in your house during the years that Atkins vilified the carbohydrate. And I'm guessing now that flexitarian diets (observing "Meatless Monday," using meat as a condiment, going vegan before 6 P.M.) are de rigueur, we'll all be buying more tofu and almond milk for a little while. As with all trendy diets, you've probably looked back at them and laughed at yourself for being such a lemming.

But here's the thing about those fads. There is usually a kernel of truth buried in each one. Even if you don't follow the Atkins diet anymore, it left you with the idea that maybe the best way to start the day was not with a Buick-size, nutritionally bankrupt bagel. And even if you abandoned that almost-vegan diet because drinking your morning coffee with soy milk was not something that should be asked of any human, you learned that a more heavily plant-based diet is something worth exploring.

What I'm saying is, even if this book doesn't wave a magic wand over dinner hour, creating a perfect tableau of happy children ingesting their wholesome meals while discussing the State of the Union, I hope a few kernels of truth will stay with you, including this one: Family dinner is worth prioritizing.

offspring sit down, open their mouths to both (a) talk to you and (b) eat. They are not dinner guests. They are not restaurant critics. They are children who need fuel in the tank. Dinner, more than anything, just has to be . . . *done*. That is where you win points in this contest.

There are recipes on pages 62-151 that are designed for any old beginner, but there are also several recipes in here that someone can make ahead of time and store in the freezer (look for "freeze ahead" instructions under recipes). So on nights when the noncook is in charge, he or she is not so much cooking as simply thawing and reheating.

But, also, as I've mentioned on my blog more than once, there are other ways the rest of the family—not just a grown-up partner in crime—can share the dinner load. The kids can go through pages 64 through 199 and pick out the recipes that appeal to them the most. (Actually, that's a nonnegotiable part of the plan.) Your kids or your noncooking partner can make a point to say, "Remember those shrimp rolls we had at the beach? Let's try that!" Your son can answer the "What do you feel like for dinner?" question with something other than pasta with butter. Anyone in the family can set the table, clear the table, unload the dishwasher, and place a bottle of ketchup on the table. I call this whole effort not "Making Dinner," but "Making Dinner Happen." Enlist the family, whoever that may be (sitter, kids, boyfriend, dogwalker), and make it happen.

RULE 3: *Spin It as an Adventure*

Whenever you decide to start your 30-Day program, make sure to carve out a moment to officially announce it to the family. Think of yourself like the late Steve Jobs launching a new Apple product. At this announcement, I suggest you not tell them the truth—that if you have to serve or eat one more soggy quesadilla dipped in ketchup, you might take the dog out for a walk one day and *never come home*. What you should do is, first, build the suspense a little. Before school drop-off, you'll say, just as they're about to shut the car door, "Your dad and I have some exciting news for you when you get home." Or, even better, you'll drop a few hints every day leading up to the announcement. "Oh, this is going to come in handy for that adventure we are planning . . . oh, did I say adventure? You'll be hearing about that later." Smile. Wink. Wink.

When it's time to make the announcement, tell them you're all going to be part of a "big exciting adventure" (use those words) and you need their help. Tell them that you want the dinner table to be the *best place ever* and the way you're going to do this is by experimenting with new meals. If they follow all the rules, and if bribery doesn't go against everything you stand for, then after thirty days, when the big exciting adventure is over, you can offer a big exciting reward, such as:

a: **A trip to the kids' favorite restaurant**
b: **One entire day when Mom and Dad can't say no**
c: **A Clean Plate Winner Certificate**
d: **A coupon to order whatever you want at the local bakery/ice cream shop/ hot dog stand/toy store**
e: **Any incentive that weakens your bribees at the knees.**

Tell them the whole goal of this is to make everyone happy and excited about what they're eating. Assure them that there will be no [fill in the

A FEW QUICK TIPS FOR PARENTS OF PICKY EATERS

*For parents who say,
"My kids will never go for this," that's fine.
But what's your other plan? What's the case for
not trying? These tips go out to you guys.*

*(There are also tons more on dinneralovestory.com—
just click the "Picky Eating" category.)*

Point and Cook

It's not an accident that this program has the kids actively involved in choosing the recipes. Have them flip through the sixty color photographs in this book or scroll through slide shows on your favorite food websites and tell you what looks good. Of course, you run the risk of its not looking exactly like the picture, but at least their heads are in the right place when they sit down to eat.

Repackage, Respin, Rebrand

Name dishes after people. (Grandma Jody's Chicken, Uncle Nick's Cauliflower, Papa's Dadoo Special . . . don't ask.) Replicate favorite restaurant dishes. (Chicken and Broccoli went from Chinese takeout MVP to most-requested meal at home as soon as we discovered how much the girls loved those soy-sauce-soaked florets.) Rechristen old ingredients: Cauliflower = White Broccoli; Swordfish = White Salmon; Brussels Sprouts = Baby Lettuce Balls.

Deconstruct

Pick new recipes that have at least one ingredient your kid likes so you can break the dinner down to individual components and feel certain that he or she won't go completely hungry . . . or ballistic. You'll be hearing more about this in a few pages.

Apply Broccoli Logic

If all else fails and the only thing you can get your kid to eat is a hot dog, keep in mind Andy's broccoli theory: No matter what the broccoli (or kale or quinoa or spinach or tofu) is sitting next to, it will magically transform the dinner into something you can feel good about feeding your children. Warning: You might have a hard time finding this concept validated in real books by real experts.

blank with something your kid detests]. But tell them also that there will be something new on the table every night and that part of the deal is that they *have to try a bite of every one of those things*. They don't have to love that bite, or even like it, but they *must* try it without fighting or whining. This is very important. Every night you debut something new at the table successfully, it's a huge boost for everyone. So you do not want to mess around with this rule. Also good to keep in mind: No one has to *love* anything. Hearing "I like it" or even "Not bad" is *major* progress. Remember: We're dealing with kids here. Success is relative!

RULE 4: *Shop Once a Week (and Take Your Kids with You)*

I know these words might strike fear into the hearts of parents with toddlers or babies, and maybe you guys can have a pass on this. Maybe. But as soon as your kids are old enough to push their own miniature shopping carts, I highly recommend taking them along. As well as your partner or spouse. This way, it sends a message that it's not on any one person's shoulders to do the shopping—and by extension the cooking—because all shoppers inevitably get tangled up in dinner planning. And beyond the more wonky benefits (your kids learn how to choose the two-ingredient pudding over the twenty-ingredient ice cream; they learn the way "junk" is insidiously positioned on the shelves right at eye level; they learn how to select the perfect limes, small and smooth-skinned; they learn marketable skills like packing grocery bags!), it cuts off so much tableside trauma at the pass. When my kids add something to the cart, they are more invested in its consumption than they would be had it just been air-dropped onto their plates. (See pages 40–41 for more tips on the weekly shop.)

RULE 5: *Build Meals Around Familiar Ingredients*

If you've spent even a minute on my blog, you know the term Deconstruction. Actually, any of you who have spent even a minute with a kid at a table already know the concept. It's the highly scientific process of separating a meal into individual components so that you might preempt any of the following complaints: It's touching! There's dressing! There's sauce! What're those green specks?!

Deconstructing Dinner has become more than a strategy at our dinner table—it's become a philosophy. I can look at almost any meal that's potentially offensive to my kids (Asian Slaw with Chicken, page 150) and break it down into parts that are actually appealing to them (chicken, peanuts, carrots). The key to this, obviously, is to make sure a few of those parts are foods that your kids are not just going to put up with eating but foods that they're *excited* about eating.

So in other words, you might want to come at dinner ideas backward. For instance, let's say your kid is a Pasta Junkie—that he spends every waking moment wondering who he has to rob in order to eat it again. Instead of wishing he would just try something else, *build* on his love for pasta. Consider making Spaghetti with Shallots and Brussels Sprouts (page 100). If he doesn't eat the Brussels sprouts, at least he'll have that positive outlook when he sits down at the table. That's what you're going for here. I find that the longer I can keep my kids' minds open, the better chance I have of getting them to try new foods.

In general, I also think it's a good idea to make sure there's always something familiar on the plate. I call this familiar ingredient "psychological latch" food, i.e., something recognizable that will always put them at ease. If you are going to be debuting a pizza that's topped with clams or poached eggs, make sure at least the other half of the pie is a classic margherita (see page 64) with a more kid-friendly "new" element like country ham or meatballs, so they're not totally taken aback. It's just not fair to spring something too exotic on them without a safety net. Unless what you're springing on them is, say, chicken Milanese. I find anything Milanese, anything with that crispy golden crust (see Buttermilk-Herb-Baked Chicken Fingers, page 192), is likely to blow their small minds.

RULE 6: *Memorize This Phrase: "I Don't Know Yet"*

You know how your kids are hardwired to ask you what's for dinner every night? It seems like an innocent question, but trust me, it has the potential to make or break your entire evening. If you tell them what you are cooking, and if what you are cooking sounds remotely weird (and anything brand-new is bound to), then your kid has a good thirty to sixty minutes to ruminate about how weird it truly is. A good thirty to sixty minutes to figure out a way to complain and beg for pizza. A good thirty to sixty minutes to start dreading his dinner instead of looking forward to it.

That's why a key strategy in your playbook is the "I Don't Know Yet" move. In other words, when one of your kids asks, "Mom, what's for dinner?" the answer is always, I repeat always, "I don't know yet." Even when you know exactly what's for dinner. Even when you are plating the fish and garnishing the black beans with cilantro. "I don't know yet."

Remember, half of what you are trying to do with this whole experiment is teach your kids the joy of *anticipating* dinner—the smells, the sizzles, the Sancerre. (Or the first two at least.) The whole idea is to preserve that romantic notion as long as possible, so there is still a little hunger-fueled excitement (as opposed to anger-fueled dread) when they finally sit down at the table.

Still skeptical that you can get the family on board

If so, just think about how easy it is to drum up excitement with kids by calling anything a contest or a challenge. Think about *Jeopardy!* If you just asked kids a bunch of questions under the category of "Geography," you think they'd be into it at all? Of course not. But assign 100 points to the question and make it a competition with other kids at a birthday party and suddenly they are all fighting to recite the fifty capitals of the United States of America in alphabetical order. You might even find that doling out prizes is not in any way necessary—that, as my mother would remind me, virtue is its own reward. I was working on this book the other day when my nine-year-old niece, Amanda, sat down on the arm of my chair and asked me to tell her what this book was about. After I summarized the challenge, her big brown eyes got bigger and she jumped up and declared, "I want to do it!" I hadn't mentioned anything about incentives. The sheer challenge aspect of it was enough.

There is one notable exception to this. If you are following Rule 5 (Build Meals Around Familiar Ingredients), then you should feel free to name that familiar ingredient in response to the question "What's for dinner?" Here's how that works:

> *Kid: Dad, what's for dinner?*
> *Parent: Pasta.*
> *Kid: Really, yum! With what?*
> *Parent: I don't know yet. But there will definitely be pasta.*

With that little decoy, you can usually get rid of nosy questioners. Then they can go off and start counting the minutes until dinner. Which is another way of saying you've got 'em right where you want 'em.

RULE 7: *Keep Notes, Keep Perspective, Keep Their Eyes on the Prize*

Before you begin Operation 30 Days, make a copy of the "Operation 30 Days Report Card" starting on page 202. (You can also download the form at dinneralovestory.com/playbook, or write directly on the pages of this book.) This will be where you and your family write down menu ideas and names of recipes that you want to try, take notes on what works and what doesn't, and give grades for everything. Notice that the blank space where you will write "Prize" is called out on the bottom. By filling out the report card every night, the kids will be eyeballing their potential reward every night, too, which will help with motivation.

Lastly, if your children's job is to try something new every day, your job is to keep a healthy perspective. The benefits from this experiment might not be apparent immediately, but I promise that even if the Slow-Cooker Korean Short Ribs (page 120) go untouched, and little noses (or big ones) scrunch at the sight of that creamy chicken soup you were so proud to execute to perfection (page 102) . . . you're getting in the habit of cooking, you're teaching your children how to make healthy choices about food, how to be open-minded, and how to respect a ritual that will bring both you and them comfort—and yes, joy—for a lifetime.

In other words: Keep your eyes on the prize.

HOW TO GET STARTED

STEP 1: *Commit*

I know it's hard to believe, but you've already accomplished the hardest part of the whole family dinner operation: committing to this challenge in the first place. I can give you all the recipes in the world; I can share my mental archive of time-saving, money-saving, sanity-saving kitchen tips; I can give you pep talks until you want to suffocate me with my pom-poms; but without the conviction to make it happen, it won't be possible. There is no magic button. Family dinner requires front-end planning, plus lots of back-end chopping and mincing and assembling. Once you realize that it's going to be a little work, once you *embrace* that work, your head will be in a much better place.

In other words, Congratulations! You've just conquered Step 1. Just by *picking up* this book, you have started down the road of making family dinner a priority.

STEP 2: *Announce!*

Again, announce Operation 30 Days to your children as though you are announcing a trip to Disney World. Don't let on that you are secretly afraid you won't be able to make it one week, let alone one month. Kids sniff out that vibe like bloodhounds. Tell them you have an exciting announcement and you will need their help. *Implicate* them, get them invested. Be enthusiastic, ambitious. Try to mention the words *adventure* and *prizes* as many times as possible. It's not bribery, it's *survival*.

Okay, maybe it's a *little* like bribery.

STEP 3: *Gather Your Recipes*

This is the fun part! Sift through the recipes in this book and all those dog-eared cookbooks, bookmarked websites, and Post-it–tagged magazines that contain recipes you've been meaning to make for so long, but, well . . . let's just say the decade got away from you. (I call this my Someday File and if you don't have one, don't worry. There are plenty of recipes to choose from on pages 62–199.) To start, you're probably going to want to pick fifteen or sixteen easy recipes I call Go-To Weeknight Meals (pages 55–151) and four or five more ambitious ones I call Keep-the-Spark-Alive Dinners (pages 165–199). The bulk of the cooking you are going to be doing during your 30-Day Mission is *weeknight* cooking and the quickest way to bring all our merriment to a screeching halt is to choose weeknight recipes that are overly involved. Anyone who has, say, found him- or herself steaming clams and whisking homemade aioli for a Rick Bayless three-shellfish paella on a Tuesday at seven o'clock while two tired, sweaty soccer players keep saying "Jeez, Mom, when are we going to *ever* eat dinner?" will have some idea what I'm talking about.

A quick story before we proceed. I was talking to my friend Erin on the soccer sidelines the other day. It was a Wednesday and she asked me what I was making for dinner. (This is my lot in life as a food blogger: Even when I'm reading the paper over morning coffee, people ask me what's on the menu ten hours later.) I told Erin I was making spaghetti with caramelized onions, spinach, and Parm—a weeknight favorite in our house because it can be pulled together in nanoseconds from even the most tumbleweed-ridden pantries.

"Oh, I don't know," she said. "My husband was going to make this recipe he found in a magazine, but now he said he's too tired to cook."

"Really?" I asked. "What was the recipe?"

"A pasta with roasted vegetables, anchovies, and bread crumbs, I think. But the bread crumbs have to be homemade and the vegetables have to be slow-roasted a certain way." She paused. "I don't know. Some recipe he found that has way too many steps for me."

Erin is married to a terrific cook, but he's someone who considers cooking dinner more like a project than a like-it-or-not family event that happens every night at seven o'clock. He is the kind of person who only feels satisfied if all four burners are fired up at once and magical, mysterious aromas are wafting throughout the house.

This is totally, obviously fine—actually, it's *wonderful*—for people who view cooking as a once-a-month project. Or for nights when you have *time* for a project. That very idea is the cornerstone of the Keep-the-Spark-Alive Dinners beginning on page 165. But this kind of cooking is totally *not fine*—not at all wonderful—for weeknights, unless you happen to live in a house where no one has anything to do all day except dream up ways you might beat Jamie Oliver in a game of *Iron Chef*. Listen closely! We are not in the business of impressing Alton Brown or our neighbors or our bosses with multicourse offerings and long lists of fancy ingredients. Again, the endgame on the weeknight is this and only this: *Put dinner on the table.*

I can't stress this enough: You will cook more regularly if you choose simple recipes. By choosing simple recipes, you will get dinner on the table more efficiently and you will not end up with a pile of dirty dishes that makes you want to chug a bottle of beta-blockers. By minimizing the prep work and the cleanup (and the beta-blockers), you will be far more likely to do it again the next night. And that is the goal. Sustainable routines. Pleasant tableside experiences. *Success*. Which for our purposes right now will be defined as "a fifteen-minute period of time during which food is consumed without drama."

In short: The best home cooks choose the easiest recipes.

Did I Say 30 Days? I Meant 20!

—

Yes, Operation 30 Days takes place over the course of one month (one delicious, exciting month!), but because I recognize that I can be a little obsessive at times (see: fifteen years of writing down what I ate for dinner), I have tweaked the program a bit since I did it, so that you do not have to make a homemade meal every night. Instead, you should feel free to cook only five nights a week, with two nights off. Those two nights can be weekends or they can be busy nights when dinner is Just. Not. An. Option. It's up to you. All I ask is that on those nights "off" you try to work in something new—spinach on the takeout pizza? a side of edamame with the chicken teriyaki? the Asian Rotisserie Chicken instead of Original Roast?—to keep the spirit of the program alive. You should feel free to go beyond twenty days, of course, but what I'm saying is that I'm flexible.

That's why when you see that two of the recipes in this cookbook are omelets (pages 114 and 140), you're not going to say, "Why do I need someone to teach me how to make a freaking omelet?" Instead, you're going to say, "Oh! I know how to make an omelet, and I am so happy you call that 'cooking.' Now what do I have to do to get myself organized for that?"

A lot of people might not consider something as pedestrian as an omelet to be "cooking dinner." But to me, it totally counts. Especially when that omelet is made with fresh eggs and served alongside a cold spring asparagus salad that doesn't need more than a few minced shallots and fresh herbs, because the spears are in season and thus require minimal intervention on the part of the cook. And therein lies another shortcut of the pros that is worth committing to memory: The fresher the ingredients,

Security Blankets

—

Some of the recipes in this book (especially the ones in the "Spark" section) might seem a little ambitious (read: scary) to kids (and therefore to their parents). To that I say, as long as you have a few security blankets on the table or waiting in the wings, you'll be able to project complete and total confidence when presenting the item in question to any tableside skeptics. So here are a few things you might want to stock up on as fallback nibbles in case, say, the tofu is a total bomb.

- *Peanut butter*
- *Whole wheat bread or pita*
- *Turkey slices*
- *Edamame*
- *Low-fat string cheese*
- *Hummus*
- *Avocado*
- *Baby carrots*

the less you have to mess with them. It's very important to recognize when to just stay out of the ingredients' way.

Now, about those multihour, four-burner, projectlike, authentic-paella-type recipes. In Operation 30 Days, these are known as Keep-the-Spark-Alive meals. Why? Because you know how, every few weeks (years?) you make a point to go out with your partner or spouse, just the two of you, to remind yourself (pretend?) that you have a life outside of your kids? These meals are the dinner versions of that idea. Even if your kids don't cheer upon their arrival, these recipes will keep the spark alive for *you* . . . the *grown-up;* they'll remind you that there is a light at the end of the tunnel and that dinner won't always mean a twirl of spaghetti with butter and a side of raw baby carrots. You won't need as many Spark meals as Go-To meals, but you'll definitely need them. I'll go into more detail in the chapter on Keep-the-Spark-Alive Dinners as to why I am convinced Spark meals saved my dinner life, but let me just say that by my calculus, if we're playing the long game here—and make no mistake about it, we are—they might just prove to be the most valuable meals of all.

STEP 4: *Make a Meal Plan*

So you have your pile of potential recipes all in one place. Now, get the family together some time before Sunday, which is the day you will go food shopping. Everyone must be present at the meeting. Bring the calendar. If your kids are older, have them bring their calendars, too. If you have young kids who might have fun filling out a calendar, by all means, let them! The point is: everyone together. All in! Pens or smartphones poised and ready for action.

Look at your collective schedules for the coming week and decide which nights will be good for Go-To Weeknight recipes (pages 55–151), when you won't have a lot of time, and which will be good for Keep-the-Spark-Alive recipes (pages 165–199), when you'll have some room for adventure. Decide who has time to cook (or thaw) on which night. Now, browse the recipes in each section (Go-To and Spark) and slot them into Week 1's schedule in the Workbook section of this book (page 201). Based on those recipes, write out a shopping list.

Sounds easy, right? Actually, there's a real science to putting together a meal plan—if you are anything like me, my heart dies a little every time I throw out half a bunch of rotten parsley. The following pages offer ten weekly meal plans, annotated to show you *why* these meals work well together in a five-day period. Hopefully at least a few will work with your family's schedule and tastebuds.

MY FORMULA FOR MAKING A MEAL PLAN

When our mothers—or maybe our mothers' mothers—were cooking for their families, they famously used monikers like Meatloaf Monday and Taco Tuesday to help them get organized. I come at it from a slightly different, if equally formulaic, angle. Most of the menu plans in the following pages will generally break down like this . . .

MEAL 1: CRAZY SIMPLE

All my dinners are easy to make,
but the ones early in the week are usually in the
Supereasy-to-Make category.
You never want to start off too ambitious—
it's all about pacing yourself mentally.

MEAL 2: MEATLESS

There's always at least one vegetarian dinner.

MEAL 3: FISH

Three's usually a seafood dinner,
which happens on Sunday or Monday, so the fish
from our weekly shop is still fresh.

MEAL 4: HALFWAY THERE

There's always one dinner that has a
make-ahead component, i.e., something that has
been prepared and frozen on the weekend,
something that has been marinating all day,
something that is based on leftovers.

MEAL 5: USE IT OR LOSE IT

The last dinner of the week is something
that takes advantage of the odds and ends of
a vegetable crisper or pantry.
Then I don't feel guilty about going out
to dinner on the weekend. (Meal 6!)

MEAL PLAN 1

Super Simple

Extra chorizo?
Freeze it
for next week.

Pulled
chicken
comes right
from the
freezer.

Classic
empty-
the-fridge
dinner

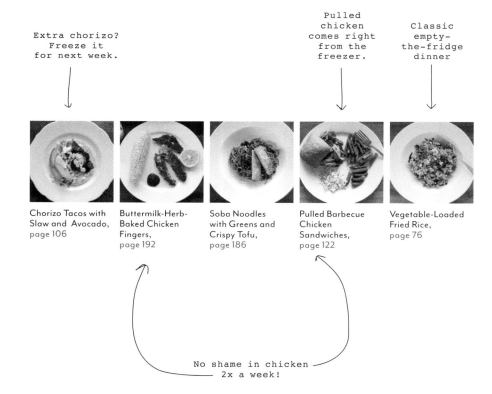

Chorizo Tacos with
Slaw and Avocado,
page 106

Buttermilk-Herb-
Baked Chicken
Fingers,
page 192

Soba Noodles
with Greens and
Crispy Tofu,
page 186

Pulled Barbecue
Chicken
Sandwiches,
page 122

Vegetable-Loaded
Fried Rice,
page 76

No shame in chicken
2x a week!

MEAL PLAN 2

My Idea of a Perfect Week

Early in the week: Don't be overly ambitious!

Pan-frying will change the way you think about pizza.

Marinate steak in the morning.

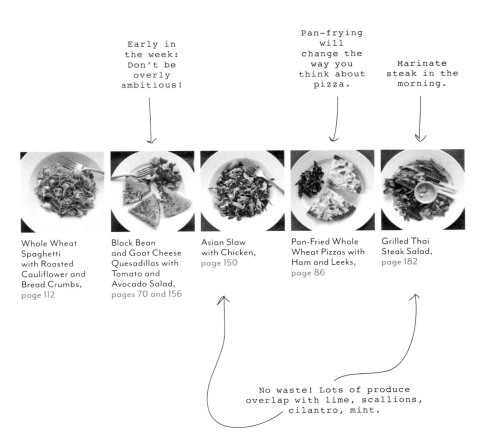

Whole Wheat Spaghetti with Roasted Cauliflower and Bread Crumbs, page 112

Black Bean and Goat Cheese Quesadillas with Tomato and Avocado Salad, pages 70 and 156

Asian Slaw with Chicken, page 150

Pan-Fried Whole Wheat Pizzas with Ham and Leeks, page 86

Grilled Thai Steak Salad, page 182

No waste! Lots of produce overlap with lime, scallions, cilantro, mint.

/ 31 /

MEAL PLAN 3

Flexitarian

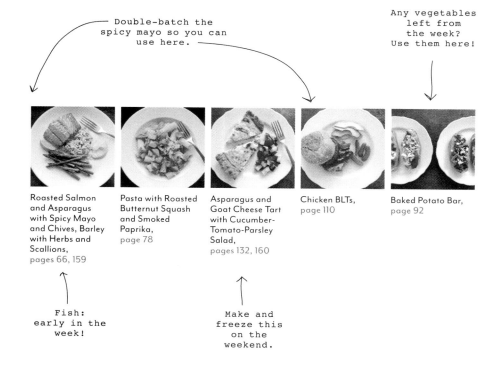

Double-batch the spicy mayo so you can use here.

Any vegetables left from the week? Use them here!

Roasted Salmon and Asparagus with Spicy Mayo and Chives, Barley with Herbs and Scallions, pages 66, 159

Pasta with Roasted Butternut Squash and Smoked Paprika, page 78

Asparagus and Goat Cheese Tart with Cucumber-Tomato-Parsley Salad, pages 132, 160

Chicken BLTs, page 110

Baked Potato Bar, page 92

Fish: early in the week!

Make and freeze this on the weekend.

MEAL PLAN 4

Quick and Strategic

Freeze This!
Money in the
Bank.

Make extra
rice to use
on these.

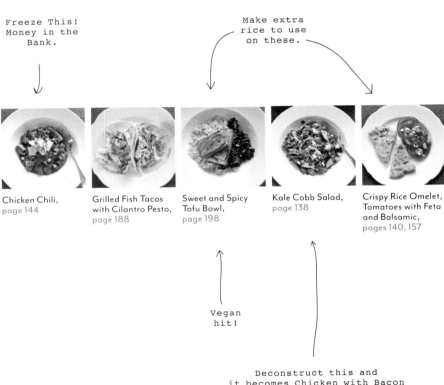

Chicken Chili,
page 144

Grilled Fish Tacos
with Cilantro Pesto,
page 188

Sweet and Spicy
Tofu Bowl,
page 198

Kale Cobb Salad,
page 138

Crispy Rice Omelet,
Tomatoes with Feta
and Balsamic,
pages 140, 157

Vegan
hit!

Deconstruct this and
it becomes Chicken with Bacon
and avocados for the kids.

MEAL PLAN 5

Summer Fresh

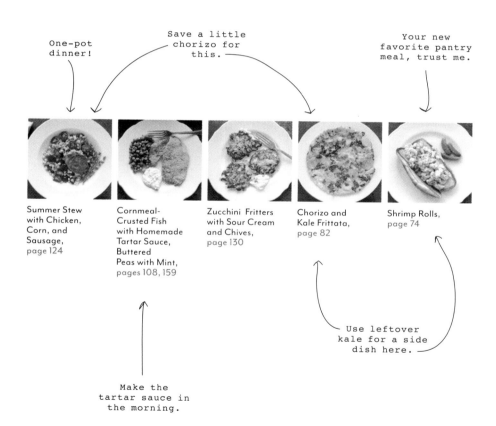

One-pot dinner!

Save a little chorizo for this.

Your new favorite pantry meal, trust me.

Summer Stew with Chicken, Corn, and Sausage, page 124

Cornmeal-Crusted Fish with Homemade Tartar Sauce, Buttered Peas with Mint, pages 108, 159

Zucchini Fritters with Sour Cream and Chives, page 130

Chorizo and Kale Frittata, page 82

Shrimp Rolls, page 74

Make the tartar sauce in the morning.

Use leftover kale for a side dish here.

MEAL PLAN 6

Super Fast

Herbs on fish and in
salad can repeat here and here.

Miso-Glazed
Salmon, Sugar
Snap Peas and
Radish Salad,
pages 104, 157

Chicken Sausages
with Kale and Slaw,
baked beans,
page 118

Basic Barbecue
Roasted Chicken,
Barley with Herbs
and Scallions,
pages 72, 159

Spinach and
Feta Omelet
with toasted
baguette,
page 114

Penne with
Roasted
Tomatoes and
Spinach,
page 80

Both of these
are faster than
any store-bought
frozen meal.

Save a few tomatoes
for the last
meal of the week.

/ 35 /

MEAL PLAN 7

Winter Warm-Your-Bones

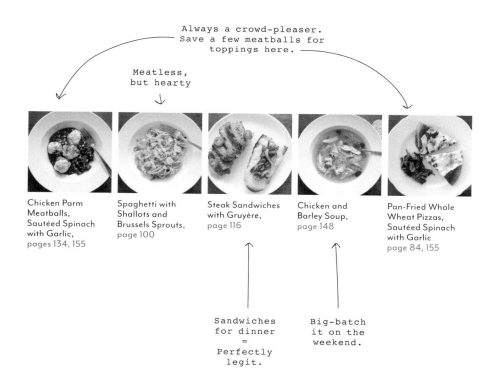

Always a crowd-pleaser.
Save a few meatballs for
toppings here.

Meatless,
but hearty

Chicken Parm
Meatballs,
Sautéed Spinach
with Garlic,
pages 134, 155

Spaghetti with
Shallots and
Brussels Sprouts,
page 100

Steak Sandwiches
with Gruyère,
page 116

Chicken and
Barley Soup,
page 148

Pan-Fried Whole
Wheat Pizzas,
Sautéed Spinach
with Garlic
page 84, 155

Sandwiches
for dinner
=
Perfectly
legit.

Big-batch
it on the
weekend.

MEAL PLAN 8

Modern Comfort Food

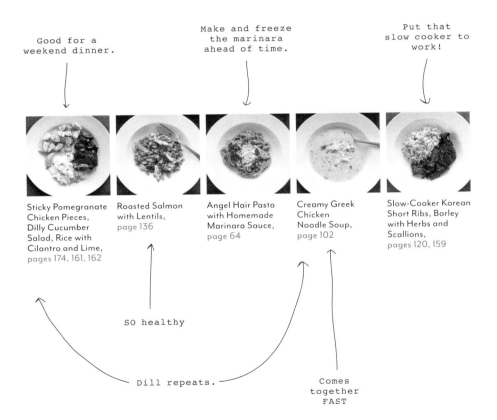

Good for a weekend dinner.

Make and freeze the marinara ahead of time.

Put that slow cooker to work!

Sticky Pomegranate Chicken Pieces, Dilly Cucumber Salad, Rice with Cilantro and Lime, pages 174, 161, 162

Roasted Salmon with Lentils, page 136

Angel Hair Pasta with Homemade Marinara Sauce, page 64

Creamy Greek Chicken Noodle Soup, page 102

Slow-Cooker Korean Short Ribs, Barley with Herbs and Scallions, pages 120, 159

SO healthy

Dill repeats.

Comes together FAST

MEAL PLAN 9

Family Faves

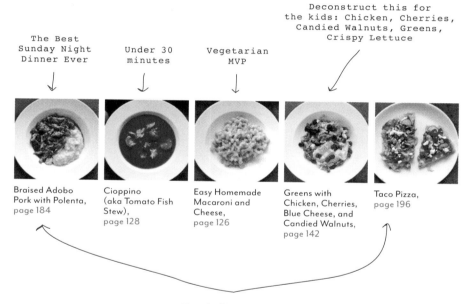

The Best Sunday Night Dinner Ever

Under 30 minutes

Vegetarian MVP

Deconstruct this for the kids: Chicken, Cherries, Candied Walnuts, Greens, Crispy Lettuce

Braised Adobo Pork with Polenta, page 184

Cioppino (aka Tomato Fish Stew), page 128

Easy Homemade Macaroni and Cheese, page 126

Greens with Chicken, Cherries, Blue Cheese, and Candied Walnuts, page 142

Taco Pizza, page 196

Use leftover pork on top of taco pizza.

MEAL PLAN 10

Classic School Nights

Not going to be arrested
for serving roasted beets
two nights in a row. (Make extra
on night one.)

Love me
a good skillet
dinner

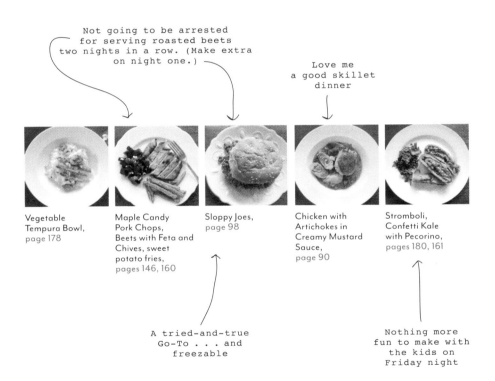

Vegetable
Tempura Bowl,
page 178

Maple Candy
Pork Chops,
Beets with Feta and
Chives, sweet
potato fries,
pages 146, 160

Sloppy Joes,
page 98

Chicken with
Artichokes in
Creamy Mustard
Sauce,
page 90

Stromboli,
Confetti Kale
with Pecorino,
pages 180, 161

A tried-and-true
Go-To . . . and
freezable

Nothing more
fun to make with
the kids on
Friday night

STEP 5: *Shop*

Every now and then I read about people who do their grocery shopping daily or nightly, letting their mood or what's fresh at the farmer's market dictate the menu. This is a wonderfully romantic notion—and also one that you should banish from your head for a little while. It doesn't mean you're going to miss out on the first ramps of spring or the sweetest corn in August. Or that I am in any way dismissing the farmer's market. (Quite the contrary—we are at ours every Saturday from June until November.) It just means that in the beginning, the bulk of your shopping list is going to be made up of things you buy at the grocery store. If you have access to a farmer's market on the weekend and can get any of those ingredients there, I would never in a million years stop you. But in the interest of keeping things manageable, I want you to make a point of shopping *once a week*. (We do ours every Sunday morning.) And that's going to be at any supermarket where you can buy good-quality produce—but also toilet paper and dog food. In the first month, we are all about streamlining. You want to eliminate as many obstacles as possible before that moment you walk in the door at night—and shopping for everything you need is one of the more enormous obstacles.

As long as we are on the subject of streamlining, I advise writing down the ingredients you need for the week (whether on your smartphone or a piece of paper) and organizing the list by aisle. If you don't have the map of the grocery store tattooed on your brain (don't worry, you will soon enough), then organize your list according to category: Produce, Dairy, Meat, Pantry. Eventually, when you find your rhythm, you will be able to do this on autopilot. Eventually you might even be like my husband. If grocery shopping were a field of study, by now he would have graduated summa cum laude and been touring the globe giving standing-room-only lectures on the topic. The man has a sixth sense for what we need. To the untrained ear, this probably sounds like a pretty great deal for me, but the reality is that it can be torturous—particularly when he somehow misses the shopping but manages to be present for the unpacking. *Did you mean to get brown rice pasta instead of whole wheat?* (No.) *Hmm, did we leave a bag in the car? Where are the snacks for lunches?* (Whoops.) *Huh, so we're going with whole yogurt for smoothies now instead of low-fat?* To preempt the postshop third degree I now take a second at the register to go through a mental list of four or five things that I always, *always* forget (drinks, snacks, toilet paper, turkey for Phoebe's lunch). I recommend you do the same—whether you live with a drill sergeant or not.

Is your list organized? Good. You are now ready to hit the supermarket—hopefully with the whole family in tow—for your Weekly Shop. It deserves uppercase letters because it is an official event that will happen every week, from here on out. Ad infinitum.

STEP 6: *Unpack and Prep for the Week*

After returning from your Weekly Shop, you obviously have to unpack your items. Easy, right? Not so fast! Unpacking is another form of organizing, and an opportunity to get ahead for the week. Before you unpack a single item, I want you to do two things. The first is what I call a "Kitchen Dump," where you repurpose the odds and ends of your fridge and fruit bowl to make room for the new crop of groceries. (See pages 42–44 for specific instructions.) The second, very important thing to do is to ask yourself, "What can I do right now to get ahead for the week?" Take a look at your dinner lineup and search for those make-ahead notes at the ends of recipes. Look for highlighted tasks that can be completed in advance—

THE ART OF THE KITCHEN DUMP

Before you hit the store for your Weekly Shop, do yourself a favor and clear some room in the refrigerator and fruit bowl for the next crop of groceries. And by clear, I do not mean discard. I mean, take a look at what's salvageable and put it to work. A few examples:

Fruit

1. I like to slice all remaining fruit (oranges, melons, apples) into grab-able pieces and place them on the kitchen table. The kids are much more likely to meet their fruit quota for the day by mindlessly picking up a sliver of apple on their way through the kitchen to the TV room than they would be if it were still whole in the fruit bowl on the counter. Shriveled berries go into storage bags in the freezer (stems cut off in the case of strawberries) for use in morning smoothies.

2. Apples covered with bruises? Peel and dice them, then fry in butter with a pinch of cinnamon for quick applesauce; or mix fried apples into pancake batter.

3. Bananas: Transfer to the freezer and use for banana bread. The skins will turn black, but this will not affect the flesh or flavor, and they'll thaw quickly.

Eggs

How annoying is one egg left in the egg carton? Really annoying. I turn it into lunch only so I can justify throwing the carton away. I make a killer egg salad sandwich, with a drop of Dijon mustard, mayo, and a few snipped chives.

Vegetables

1. Blanch broccoli or slice bell peppers (or in my case, slice the three or four bell pepper halves . . . what the?) and pack them in little containers to throw into lunch boxes throughout the week.

2. Tomatoes: Even if they are as shriveled as gremlins, you can save them with a slow roast. Preheat the oven to 300°F. Place

however many grape or cherry tomatoes you have on a foil- or parchment-lined rimmed baking sheet, and drizzle with olive oil and a little honey. Sprinkle with salt and pepper. Roast for 1 to 1½ hours, until golden and slightly bursting, and store in an airtight container for up to three days. Then use them in eggs, tossed into whole-grain salads, or layer with ricotta cheese on top of toasted baguette slices for breakfast pizzas or after-school snacks.

3. Wilting vegetables: Dump flaccid carrots, peppers, beans, onions, celery, herbs—virtually anything that isn't covered with mold—into a large pot of water with salt, pepper, and a Parmesan rind (if you have it), and simmer for an hour. Strain in a colander for a quick vegetable broth. Use the broth to impart flavor where you usually just use water: boiling pastas, making soups, steaming vegetables, cooking grains.

Chicken Broth
Cartons of broth half full? Empty them into ice trays, freeze, and then store the cubes in a plastic freezer bag. These come in so handy for popping into a pot of water for extra flavor when making grains, pastas, or vegetables.

Herbs
Whirl in a blender with yogurt, olive oil, half an onion, salt, and pepper. Use as a marinade for chicken, shrimp, or lamb.

Team Family Dinner

You know how every sports team your kids play for has some kind of team manager who sends around e-mails with details about the next practice, the next opponent, the location of the game, and whether to wear blue or white? That's what you have to be for Team Family Dinner. You have to be thinking about how it will happen and how to get people there in spite of everything—sports, homework, commuting—conspiring against it. You have to be Family Dinner's Team Manager. Give it the same weight you'd give the lacrosse team if twenty-three kids were relying on you, and I guarantee a winning streak at the table.

either in the morning before you go to work or on the weekend when you have a little time to stock up on some dinner building blocks, like a batch of whole grains or a marinara sauce. Pick two or three things to do (or as many as you have time for) immediately following the unpacking. What you choose to get a head start on is your decision, but I favor any of the tasks listed on pages 50–53.

STEP 7: *Follow Your Own Orders*

When you wake up on Monday morning, look at your schedule to see what's on the lineup for the night's dinner. Is there anything you can prep before you go to work (look for the make-ahead note) that you haven't already done on the weekend? Can you chop an onion, set a pot of water on the stovetop (small, but somehow *incredibly* satisfying to walk in and just turn the heat to high), marinate some pork, transfer a piece of meat from the freezer to the refrigerator? Whatever you can get done before you leave for work will be appreciated like you wouldn't *believe* at the other end of the day.

STEP 8: *Dinner!*

By this point you might be scratching your head and thinking, "How come there are seven steps and thirty pages devoted to organizing and planning and prepping and getting pumped for dinner and only one step devoted to the actual making of dinner?"

Is a lightbulb going off in your head right now?

That feeling of dread you have been known to associate with dinner? Is it gone just a little bit? I hope it is. Because if you've followed the first

Can I Skip That?

At some point in this book you're going to come across an ingredient that (a) you've never cooked with, (b) intimidates you, and (c) you think you can probably skip with no harm done. If the budget allows, I would like to take this opportunity to argue against that. You'll see that once you have these flavor-blasters in your pantry, you'll (a) notice them in more places, (b) be more willing to try recipes in which they appear, and (c) wonder why it took you so long to discover them in the first place.

- Anchovies
- Canned chipotles in adobo
- Chile paste
- Cider vinegar
- Fennel seeds
- Fish sauce
- Hoisin
- Hot sauce
- Miso
- Prepared horseradish
- Rice wine vinegar
- Smoked paprika
- Sriracha

seven steps, the hardest part of dinner—the planning, the think-work, maybe even some of the herb-washing—is behind you. If you've followed the first seven steps, you know exactly what's on the menu so there's none of that what-to-make agita that can crush the strongest among us at the end of a workday. You've prepped an ingredient or two in advance so the momentum is already on your side. All you have to do is close the deal. And cook the meal. And have a glass of wine if that's your thing. And order the kids to set the table. And eat. Together.

STEP 9: *Fill Out Your Chart*

After you've all enjoyed your meal (remember: The term "enjoyed" can be broadly interpreted here), take a minute to fill out the rest of the workbook chart. What grade would you give it? What grade do the kids give it? Take into account any or all of the following: Did it require too much prep? Were there tears (yours or theirs)? Was the cleanup brutal? Was it deconstructable for picky eaters? And finally, perhaps, most crucially: Was it a keeper? Will you make it again? That's the Holy Grail.

A Note About Make-Ahead

—

You might take a look at all my suggestions for getting ahead of the game and say, "Oh, that's crazy. Whisking a vinaigrette takes three minutes. Assembling nonperishable dinner ingredients on the counter before I leave for work takes one. I don't have to do that stuff ahead of time. I can just as easily take care of all that when I walk in the door later on today."

That's fine, of course. Who am I to tell you what to do?

All I'm suggesting here is that when it comes to family dinner, I like to remove as many variables as possible because, as we all know, it's just so much easier to skip cooking, to look for any excuse to pick up the phone and order takeout, or heat up a third frozen pizza in three days. If you've been slowly checking things off the to-do list—no matter how small—they'll all add up to protection against that temptation.

And anyway, if you are like me, you are most likely a different animal after work than you are before work. Before work, I open the fridge and hear angels singing. Every vegetable seems to glow with promise. After work—which is to say after commuting back and forth to the city, after dealing with coworkers who aren't exactly prioritizing my family dinner the way I am, after nagging about the homework, supervising the vocabulary, running through fifty flash cards and all the single-digit times tables, and picking up a kid at soccer on the other side of the county, after emptying the somehow-still-full lunch box from earlier in the day—what I see in the fridge is a bunch of unrelated ingredients that add up to nothing, that taunt me from the shelves. But that's just me.

Your post-work self might be a lot smarter.

PREP FOR THE WEEK

I know I'm repeating myself here, but this is arguably the most crucial step of the entire operation. Why? Because you are training yourself to think ahead for the week. You are organizing, prioritizing, and getting the momentum going. You are—here's that word again—committing. Once you have a jar of homemade vinaigrette in the refrigerator, you are much more likely to put it to use later on in the week. Once you have a batch of meatballs in the freezer, I'm telling you, all week long you will be dreaming about the day you get to walk in the door after work, heat them up with some sauce for Chicken Parm Meatballs (page 134), pour yourself a glass of Pinot, and sit down with the kids for a homemade meal. Without breaking a sweat. Without all the attendant anxiety that you might be used to around dinnertime. Slowly, very slowly, if you chip away at the front-end work little by little, you'll see that dinner can become a source of pleasure, not pain. Here are a few things to get out of the way on the weekend:

Make a vinaigrette.
It's impossible to overstate the magic that happens when you have a stash of this in the fridge just waiting to kick up greens and grain salads. What's wrong with the bottled vinaigrettes you get in the store? Nothing really—if you're not buying the ones with all those additives. I think the house I grew up in was single-handedly responsible for keeping Newman's Own in business. But once I got in the habit of making my own homemade dressings and storing them in a jam jar, I got addicted to a certain brightness that you just can't find in the bottles, no matter how fresh they claim to be. I always say, if the only homemade thing on the table is a vinaigrette, your dinner's still gonna sing.

Basic Vinaigrette
In an old jam jar shake the following ingredients:
- heaping ½ teaspoon Dijon mustard
- ¼ cup cider vinegar
  (or red or white wine vinegar)
- 1 teaspoon sugar
- salt and pepper
- squeeze of fresh lemon juice

Then add:
- ⅓ cup extra-virgin olive oil

Shake again. Store in the refrigerator for up to two weeks.

Roast and shred some chicken breasts.
All kinds of possibilities suddenly present themselves to me when I have shredded chicken in the bank: Kale Cobb Salad (page 138), Greens with Chicken, Cherries, Blue Cheese, and Candied Walnuts (page 142), Creamy Greek Chicken Noodle Soup (page 102), chicken salad on a croissant. (Oh man, oh man, oh man, how much do I love that sandwich?) How to prep your chicken: Place 2 or 3 split chicken breasts or boneless chicken breasts on a foil-lined rimmed baking sheet. Pour in ¼ cup water and tent with foil. Roast at 375°F for 40 minutes. Bone-in split breasts are good for shredding; boneless breasts are good for slicing on the bias. Cool, shred with two forks, wrap in foil, and refrigerate for up to 3 days.

Make a batch of whole grains (quinoa, barley, rice).
You know what they say in soccer: The best offense is a good defense. Same thing here. Having a batch of healthy carbs ready to go is the best way to protect yourself against the instinct to fall back on side dishes that are devoid of nutritional merit like French fries, dinner rolls, and baguettes. (Baguettes, by the way, are my great weakness. It is unthinkable for me to have soup without a good crusty white baguette alongside it, so be prepared to call me on my hypocrisy a few chapters down the road.)

Basic quinoa instructions:
Bring 2 cups water to a boil in a medium saucepan. Add 1 cup quinoa and simmer, covered, until tender, fluffy, and water is absorbed—about 15

minutes. Let stand, covered, off the heat for 5 minutes, then fluff with a fork. Yields about 3 cups cooked quinoa.

Basic barley instructions:
Bring 1 cup pearl barley that has been rinsed and picked over, 1 teaspoon salt, and 3 cups water to a boil in a medium pot. Cover and simmer for 50 minutes, or until the barley is firm but cooked through. Makes 3 cups barley.

Blanch broccoli or green beans so you can easily toss them into a salad or a stir-fry.
To make: Immerse the vegetables in simmering water for 3 to 4 minutes, then remove the vegetables with a mesh strainer and immediately plunge them into a bowl of ice water to stop the cooking and preserve the bright green color. Drain well and pat dry with paper towels. Store in a sealed container in the refrigerator.

Wash greens and herbs.
This is one of those tasks that, for whatever reason, fills me with dread. The rinsing-spinning-drying routine is just the kind of thing that sinks my heart on a weeknight. But on the weekend, when I have ten minutes between soccer games (or, back in the day, when the girls were simultaneously napping, hallelujah!), it's such a no-brainer to cross off the list. Washed greens will last a few days wrapped loosely in a paper towel and stored in an open plastic bag.

GO-TO WEEKNIGHT MEALS

Once, while sitting in creaky fold-out sideline chairs watching our nine-year-old girls play lacrosse—at the very dinner-unfriendly hour of 7:00 P.M.—another mother, a pediatrician, told me that her husband accused her of being "obsessed with food." To which she responded, "I'm not obsessed with food. I'm just obsessed with food *planning*."

I think about this conversation all the time—because I am obsessed with food planning, too, and because, to be honest, I don't really know how you *can't* be if you have any **desire to crack the weeknight family dinner code.** As much as it pains me to concede this, I am no longer a twentysomething college grad, content to live on 🥚 hard-boiled eggs and Boca Burgers, responsible for only myself. I assume you aren't either.

This section is called "Go-To Weeknight Meals," which is another way of saying Weeknight Recipes, which is another way of saying that this is where you are going to learn how to become obsessed with food planning—and I mean that in the best possible way. There are **tons of great recipes** in the following pages that can be made from start to finish with minimal fuss and energy when you walk in the door in the evening. Recipes that are so easy, in fact, that, while assembling them, you will be able to focus on your kids' complicated tales of cafeteria politics or help with math homework from across the kitchen (even fractions!). All of the meals in this section troubleshoot family dinner in some way, meaning that they're super-quick to put together, they can be deconstructed so the kids can pick and choose which parts they like, or they're conducive to being **made ahead**—and I hope you'll find yourself returning to them over and over, even when your dinner challenge is a distant memory (and when you are, presumably, in the phase where you raise a glass 🍷 to me every night in gratitude for setting you down the right path). The recipes here are **fast, healthy, and basic—many of them the kinds of dishes you feel like you should probably already know how to make by this point in your life.**

But the goal of this chapter is not only to bulk up your archive of thirty-minute recipes. It's to teach you (how to organize) yourself so that when you walk into your kitchen every night, you are already halfway done with the think-work and the prep work (i.e., the *hard* work) and you can actually, honest-to-god feel relaxed about the cooking that is about to transpire. By the time you sit down at your table, with your sweet, sweaty charges sitting around **like squeaky birds with their mouths wide open**, waiting to be fed, you'll be unwound and ready to sink into a little therapeutic downtime after a day filled with chaos. **Happy chaos.** But chaos nonetheless.

➡ The first step toward achieving obsessive food planning status is getting in the habit of asking yourself this question once or twice a day: "What can I do right now to make my weeknight dinners easier?" In the beginning, you might have to force it. It might feel odd thinking about Tuesday's dinner on Sunday, or organizing yourself for braised short ribs in between reading sections of the morning paper. But once you see how much it streamlines your dinner hour, **planning ahead will become addictive.** It's like having your own sous-chef. Granted, it's you who's doing both the sous-cheffing and the cheffing, but I'm telling you—it works.

There are a few specific times you should remember to ask yourself the **"What can I do right now?"** question. As you've read in the previous section, the first time is on the weekend, preferably right when you return from your Weekly Shop. **Saturday and Sunday** are when you will most likely have chunks of time to complete medium to medium-large make-ahead, cooking tasks. On those days, you can, to review: make a vinaigrette (one step closer to the Asian Slaw with Chicken on page 150); simmer a marinara (one step closer to Angel Hair Pasta with Homemade Marinara Sauce, page 64, or Pan-Fried Whole Wheat Pizzas, page 84); concoct some homemade barbecue sauce (one step closer to Pulled Barbecue Chicken Sandwiches, page 122); bake and freeze an Asparagus and Goat Cheese Tart (page 132); chop or blanch vegetables (one step closer to Vegetable Tempura Bowl, page 178); make peanut dressing (one step closer to Grilled Thai Steak Salad, page 182); or whirl a yogurt sauce in the blender (one step closer to Chorizo Tacos with Slaw and Avocado, page 106). You can even bake a fleet of meatballs in the same amount of time it takes your helpers (you will enlist helpers, right?) to put away the groceries. (See Chicken Parm Meatballs, page 134.) All of these tasks will leave you with substantial building blocks for dinner, if not dinner in its entirety, to use over the next few days.

There is another crucial time to ask, **"What can I do right now to make my weeknight dinners easier?"** And that is in the morning right before you leave for work or wherever your day is going to take you. Throughout this section, you'll see suggestions below recipes that indicate prep tasks that are smaller than the ones you'd do on the weekend but serve the same purpose: **to get one step ahead 🠖 of the game.**

And when I say small tasks, I mean small: assembling all your ingredients on the counter (so you won't have to root around for tamari in the pantry later in the day only to realize you have barely a drop left); washing herbs, chopping an onion; transferring frozen meat to the fridge; marinating pork chops in soy sauce, maple syrup, rice wine vinegar, and a chunk of ginger (Maple Candy Pork Chops, page 146). Each of these things takes under one minute, but they serve a larger purpose: They get the ball rolling on dinner and they force you to decide what the meal is— which, for me, is the hardest part of the whole operation. If you're lucky, checking these things off the list also might give you the (delusional) idea that you have some semblance of control over your life. Throughout this section you'll see notes underneath select recipes that highlight things that can be done on the weekend or in the morning. Use them!

No matter when you're completing your make-ahead tasks and no matter how much you want to curse my name when the shoes need to be tied in time to make the morning school bus and there you are, chopping a freaking onion, it's important to keep in mind what you are doing here. You are training yourself to think like a food planner. And if you chip away at the prep here and there, little by little, instead of starting from zero every night, if you come up with a plan to stick to, the whole idea of family dinner will start to feel a little less overwhelming. It's possible you might even be **psyched to do it all again tomorrow.**

OK, WHY EXACTLY
ARE YOU DOING THIS AGAIN?
A QUICK SUMMARY . . .

- **To break out of your dinner rut.**

- To add new, delicious meals to your repertoire that you feel confident cooking.

- **To learn how to organize, shop, and plan for dinner. (Related: To avoid the self-loathing that results from staring at a full refrigerator but having no earthly idea what to make.)**

- To discover a little of your pre-parent self, the person who was actually excited about cooking.

- **Or, if you just laughed at this description (because are you kidding? You were never that person to begin with), to teach you how to be excited about cooking.**

- To know exactly what is going into your children's bodies. Well, at least for those hours they're not in school, trading their snack-time apricots for three green Skittles.

- **To teach your kids how to try new things without checking yourself into a mental hospital.**

- To kick-start a family ritual that will pay back in beautiful, delicious dividends for many years to come.

GO-TO WEEKNIGHT MEALS: THE LINEUP

Angel Hair Pasta with Homemade Marinara Sauce
64

Roasted Salmon and Asparagus with Spicy Mayo and Chives
66

Pan-Roasted Chicken Thighs with Potato-Carrot Hash
68

Black Bean and Goat Cheese Quesadillas
70

Basic Barbecue Roasted Chicken
72

Shrimp Rolls
74

Vegetable-Loaded Fried Rice
76

Pasta with Roasted Butternut Squash and Smoked Paprika
78

Penne with Roasted Tomatoes and Spinach
80

Chorizo and Kale Frittata
82

Pan-Fried Whole Wheat Pizzas
84

Pan-Fried Whole Wheat Pizzas with Ham and Leeks
86

Hoisin Turkey Burgers
88

Chicken with Artichokes in Creamy Mustard Sauce
90

Baked Potato Bar
92

Pasta with Peas, Bacon, and Ricotta
94

Grilled Chicken with Peanut Curry Sauce
96

Sloppy Joes
98

Spaghetti with Shallots and Brussels Sprouts
100

Creamy Greek Chicken Noodle Soup
102

Miso-Glazed Salmon
104

Chorizo Tacos with Slaw and Avocado
106

Cornmeal-Crusted Fish with Homemade Tartar Sauce
108

Chicken BLTs
110

Whole Wheat Spaghetti with Roasted Cauliflower and Bread Crumbs
112

Spinach and Feta Omelet
114

Steak Sandwiches with Gruyère
116

Chicken Sausages with Kale Slaw
118

Slow-Cooker Korean Short Ribs
120

Pulled Barbecue Chicken Sandwiches
122

Summer Stew with Chicken, Corn, and Sausage
124

Easy Homemade Macaroni and Cheese
126

Cioppino (aka Tomato Fish Stew)
128

Zucchini Fritters with Sour Cream and Chives
130

Asparagus and Goat Cheese Tart
132

Chicken Parm Meatballs
134

Roasted Salmon with Lentils
136

Kale Cobb Salad
138

Crispy Rice Omelet
140

Greens with Chicken, Cherries, Blue Cheese, and Candied Walnuts
142

Chicken Chili
144

Maple Candy Pork Chops
146

Chicken and Barley Soup
148

Asian Slaw with Chicken
150

Unless otherwise noted, all recipes serve four.

ANGEL HAIR PASTA
with HOMEMADE MARINARA SAUCE

I'm starting with this recipe because everyone should know how to make a basic marinara sauce. It's the ultimate dinner building block and can be the base for so many meals—pasta, meatballs, pizzas. Commit it to memory and it'll come together faster than your kids can watch one SpongeBob episode on a Saturday morning.

Time: 35 minutes

¼ cup olive oil, plus more for coating the pasta

3 heaping tablespoons finely chopped onion (about ½ small onion)

1 garlic clove, minced (2 cloves if you are a garlic lover)

salt and pepper to taste

1 tablespoon dried oregano

quick shake of red pepper flakes (go easy on this if your kids aren't fans of heat)

2 teaspoons sugar

2 tablespoons tomato paste

1 28-ounce can tomato puree

1 pound angel hair pasta

Parmesan, freshly grated to taste, but don't be stingy

▸ Set a medium saucepan over medium heat. Add the olive oil and onions and cook until the onions have softened, about 3 minutes. Add the garlic, salt and pepper, oregano, and red pepper flakes and cook for another minute, watching closely so the garlic doesn't burn. Add the sugar and smush in the tomato paste with ¼ cup water until all the onions are coated in tomato. Stir in the tomato puree and bring to a boil. Reduce the heat and simmer uncovered for 20 to 25 minutes.

▸ Prepare the pasta according to the package directions. After draining, return the pasta to the pot with a drizzle of olive oil and toss with a spoonful of the marinara.

▸ Serve the pasta topped with the remaining marinara and lots of Parmesan.

Suggested side: Sautéed Spinach with Garlic (page 155)
On the weekend: Make your marinara.
To store: Store cooled sauce in an airtight container in the fridge. Use or freeze within 5 days. Add a little water to the reheated sauce to reach the right consistency.
To freeze: Allow the sauce to cool, then store it in a zip-lock freezer bag. Flatten the bag and seal it with as little air inside as possible. It will keep in the freezer for 3 months.
To reheat: Thaw the frozen sauce under cool running water before squeezing it into a pot set over low heat.
In the morning: Chop your onion and store in the fridge covered; set out all the nonperishable ingredients on the counter.

If you have leftover sauce, freeze it in ziplock bags and use for meatball sandwiches, homemade pizza, or another round of pasta.

ROASTED SALMON *and* ASPARAGUS *with* SPICY MAYO *and* CHIVES

This recipe is for any parent interested in expanding his or her children's dipping repertoire beyond ketchup. (Decoded: Pretty sure this is for everyone!) The Sriracha–spiked mayo has some serious umami action, without being too spicy, and takes seconds to come together.

Time: 30 minutes

2 tablespoons olive oil

2 tablespoons fresh
lemon juice

1 tablespoon honey

salt to taste

1½ pounds salmon
fillets, cut into 4
6-ounce pieces

1 bunch of asparagus,
trimmed, chopped
and tossed with olive oil,
salt, and pepper

⅓ cup mayonnaise

2 teaspoons Sriracha
(or to taste)

1 teaspoon chopped
fresh chives, plus more
for garnish

▸ Preheat the oven to 400°F.

▸ In a small bowl, whisk together the olive oil, lemon juice, honey, and salt. In a shallow roasting pan or rimmed baking sheet, nestle the fillets among the prepared asparagus pieces, brush with the olive oil mixture, and roast for 10 to 15 minutes, until the salmon is cooked through and the asparagus looks crispy but not burned.

▸ Meanwhile, in a small bowl stir together the mayonnaise, Sriracha, and chives. Serve the salmon and asparagus with a dollop of the sauce on the side. Garnish everything with more chives.

In the morning: Make your dip and trim the asparagus. Refrigerate.
Suggested side: Barley with Herbs and Scallions (page 159)

PAN-ROASTED CHICKEN THIGHS *with* POTATO-CARROT HASH

*A version of this dish was one of the first complete meals
I ever learned how to make—from watching my own mother do it.
Make sure you use an ovenproof skillet—such as a cast-iron
pan—for the chicken and chop your vegetables into small, uniform
pieces so they cook more quickly and evenly.*

Time: 30 minutes

1 cup carrots, finely diced

1½ cups red or Yukon Gold potatoes, finely diced

1 onion, roughly chopped

leaves from 4 or 5 fresh thyme sprigs

salt and pepper to taste

5 tablespoons olive oil

1½ pounds boneless chicken thighs

1 teaspoon sweet paprika

juice from ½ lemon (optional)

▸ Preheat the oven to 450°F.

▸ In a 9-by-9-inch roasting pan lined with foil, combine the carrots, potatoes, onions, and thyme. Season with salt and pepper, drizzle with 3 tablespoons of the olive oil, and gently toss to coat the vegetables. Place in the oven.

▸ Season the chicken with salt, pepper, and the paprika. Heat the remaining 2 tablespoons of oil in a large oven-proof skillet set over high heat. Add the chicken to the skillet, skin side down, and cook for 2 minutes. Reduce the heat to medium-high and cook for another 10 minutes or so, until the skin is golden brown.

▸ Flip the chicken, then transfer the skillet to the oven alongside the vegetables. (Give the vegetables a toss at this point.)

▸ Roast for another 15 minutes, or until the chicken is cooked through and the vegetables are tender. Everything should be ready at about the same time. Squeeze the lemon on top of the chicken, if desired.

In the morning: Transfer your chicken to the fridge to thaw if it's in the freezer (if it's one huge chunk of stuck-together chicken, do your best to separate the pieces so they thaw more quickly); chop the onions or carrots, or both. Chop the potatoes and submerge them in a bowl of water, which will prevent them from turning brown. Suggested sides: Sandwich Slaw (page 162) or Cucumber-Tomato-Parsley Salad (page 160)

I like dolloping some chutney on the side to add a little kick, but if you think that's pushing it with the kids, feel free to pretend I never said that.

/ 69 /

BLACK BEAN
and GOAT CHEESE
QUESADILLAS

My girls aren't goat cheese lovers, so for their quesadillas, I'll use shredded Cheddar or Jack. The important thing here is to get the kids on board with black beans. There are so many healthy dinner directions you can go once you have beans in the wheelhouse—so to me, it's worth any time and tears. This recipe makes five super-stuffed quesadillas. I recommend cutting them into pizza wedges and serving on a large platter.

Time: 25 minutes

2 tablespoons
vegetable oil

2 garlic cloves,
finely chopped

1 teaspoon ground
cumin

2 15-ounce cans
black beans, rinsed
and drained

salt and pepper to taste

3 scallions
(white and light green
parts only), chopped

5 8-inch whole
wheat tortillas

5 ounces goat cheese

salsa or salsa verde,
for dipping

▶ In a large skillet, heat the oil over medium heat. Add the garlic and cumin and stir until the garlic is golden, about 1 minute. Stir in the beans, salt, and pepper, mashing everything with a large fork. Add ⅓ cup water and the scallions and cook, stirring until most of the water is absorbed, 2 to 3 minutes. Remove from the heat.

▶ Set a separate skillet over medium-high heat and add a shot of cooking spray. Place one tortilla in the skillet, spreading about a fifth of the bean filling on one side. Sprinkle a fifth of the goat cheese on top of the beans and fold the other half of the tortilla over to seal. Flip around a few times until the tortilla is golden on both sides and the cheese is melted, 2 to 3 minutes. Remove to a dinner plate and tent with foil to keep warm. Repeat with the remaining tortillas. Cut each into three or four wedges and serve with salsa or salsa verde.

Suggested side: Rice with Cilantro and Lime (page 162); or Tomato and Avocado Salad (page 156)

BASIC BARBECUE ROASTED CHICKEN

I love sharing this recipe with parents who claim they don't know how to cook. I'll argue it's as easy as throwing chicken nuggets into the oven—and way more delicious. Using store-bought barbecue sauce is kind of cheating, yes. But that's OK. As soon as you get the hang of the technique you can start making your own.

Time: 40 minutes

2 pounds chicken pieces (drumsticks and thighs or both), salted and peppered

¾ cup Homemade Barbecue Sauce (see box below) or your favorite store-bought barbecue sauce

▸ Preheat the oven to 425°F.

▸ Place the chicken on a foil-lined roasting pan. Brush a thin layer of barbecue sauce on each piece of chicken. Bake for 10 minutes. Flip the chicken and brush another thin layer of sauce on each piece. After another 10 minutes, repeat. Discard any unused barbecue sauce.

▸ After the chicken pieces have baked for about 30 minutes total, they are done. (The juice should run clear when the chicken is pricked with a knife.)

▸ If anyone likes their chicken on the saucy side, add another layer of sauce before serving. Otherwise, you're done. I swear. That's it.

Suggested side: Whole Grains with Vegetables (page 158)
On the weekend: Make your own barbecue sauce!
In the morning: Transfer your chicken to the fridge to thaw if it's in the freezer.

HOMEMADE BARBECUE SAUCE

This is one of those witch's-brew type recipes that an older kid might have fun mixing up on the stovetop—so put 'em to work. If you make extra sauce, it keeps in the fridge for up to three weeks and works well with ribs and pork tenderloin, too.

Time: 15 minutes · 2 teaspoons Worcestershire sauce · 1 shot bourbon (optional) ⅓ cup cider vinegar · 3 tablespoons Dijon mustard · 1 garlic clove, minced ¼ small onion, chopped · ½ cup ketchup · ½ cup light brown sugar, unpacked · ¼ cup molasses · salt and pepper to taste · ¼ teaspoon ground cumin · 1 dried chile pepper

In a small saucepan over medium heat, combine all of the ingredients. Cook for 7 to 8 minutes, stirring occasionally, until thickened. Remove from the heat and let cool. Remove chile pepper, transfer to a blender, and blend until smooth. Add water, a tablespoon at a time, if you like a thinner sauce.

SHRIMP ROLLS

I used to make these sandwiches only during the summer and only when we had access to fresh shrimp. But once I realized how much the kids loved them—and once I began noticing how many options there were for good-quality shelled wild shrimp in the freezer aisle— I started folding them into the year-round dinner routine.

Time: 20 minutes

1¾ pounds
medium shrimp
(buy them shelled)

¼ cup mayonnaise

1 small celery stalk,
peeled and finely
chopped

2 teaspoons prepared
horseradish

4 scallions
(light green and white
parts only), chopped

1 tablespoon fresh
lemon juice

1 tablespoon
red wine vinegar

¼ teaspoon paprika

salt and pepper to taste

1 tablespoon fresh dill,
chopped

6 hot dog buns,
preferably potato rolls

butter, at room
temperature

▸ Bring a large pot of water to a boil. Add the shrimp and cook until the water returns to a boil, about 4 minutes. Drain the shrimp and rinse them with cold water. Once they are cool enough to handle, chop them into bite-size pieces.

▸ In a large bowl, whisk together the mayonnaise, celery stalk, horseradish, scallions, lemon juice, vinegar, paprika, salt and pepper, and dill. (If you have time to chill the salad, cover the bowl and place it in the refrigerator for as long as you've got, and up to one day). When you are ready to eat, toast the hot dog buns and spread each with a thin layer of butter. Top with shrimp salad.

Suggested sides: Corn with Butter and Cotija Cheese (page 157) or corn on the cob; Halved Avocado with Vinaigrette (page 156)
In the morning or on the weekend: Take 15 minutes to cook your shrimp. Or, at the very least, transfer your shrimp from the freezer to the fridge if they're frozen, so they're thawed come dinnertime.

This recipe makes six sandwiches: two for each grown-up, one for each kid.

VEGETABLE-LOADED FRIED RICE

This meal is excellent at the
end of a week when you're trying to use up
all those vegetable odds and ends.
I encourage you to be creative with ingredients
here—there are no wrong answers!

Time: 30 minutes

2 tablespoons neutral oil such as canola, coconut, or vegetable

2 teaspoons sesame oil

¼ small onion, chopped (about 3 tablespoons)

1 teaspoon peeled, minced fresh ginger

1 garlic clove, minced

3 cups cooked brown rice

3 eggs, whisked

3 tablespoons low-sodium soy sauce (or to taste)

2 cups vegetables (such as shredded red cabbage, chopped bell pepper, peas, precooked broccoli, shelled edamame, chopped snap peas, chopped carrots, corn, cooked zucchini)

Sriracha to taste (optional)

handful of fresh cilantro leaves, chopped

▶ Add the oils to a large skillet set over medium heat. Add the onions, ginger, and garlic and cook until the onions are slightly softened, about 1 minute. Turn the heat to medium-high and add the rice in one layer so as many of the grains as possible are crisping on the hot pan's surface. Cook for about 1 minute, stirring once after 30 seconds. Push the rice to the perimeter of the pan and add the eggs to the center, scrambling with your spoon and gradually pulling rice into the eggs as they cook. Stir in the soy sauce and cook for another minute, or until everything is integrated.

▶ Add the vegetables and cook until everything is heated through, about another minute.

▶ Drizzle with Sriracha, if desired, and sprinkle with cilantro.

On the weekend: Make the brown rice and store in the refrigerator in a covered bowl.
In the morning: Chop the onion, mince the ginger, and store them, covered, in the refrigerator; assemble the nonperishable ingredients on the counter.

PASTA *with* ROASTED BUTTERNUT SQUASH *and* SMOKED PAPRIKA

I would live on this recipe if it weren't for the small fact that my eldest dislikes pasta. It's perfect for a fall weeknight. Warning: Smoked paprika is intense, so no matter how much you like the flavor here, don't give in to the temptation to use more than called for.

Time: 35 minutes

3 cups (about 24 ounces) chopped butternut squash (or 1 large squash that has been peeled, seeded, and chopped; but I implore you: buy it already chopped)

½ onion, chopped

leaves from 4 or 5 fresh thyme sprigs

3 tablespoons olive oil

salt and pepper to taste

2 teaspoons smoked paprika

1 pound any pasta (I like pappardelle or penne)

½ cup freshly grated Parmesan, plus more for serving

fresh ricotta (optional), for serving

▶ Preheat the oven to 425°F.

▶ In a baking dish lined with foil, toss together the squash, onions, thyme, olive oil, salt and pepper, and paprika. Roast for about 30 minutes, or until the squash is brown around the edges and is tender when pierced with a fork.

▶ Meanwhile, prepare the pasta according to the package directions, reserving ¼ cup of pasta water before draining.

▶ Return the drained pasta to the pot and toss with the squash.

▶ Add the Parmesan with half of the reserved pasta water to thin and evenly distribute the cheese. Add the remaining pasta water if needed. Serve topped with more Parmesan and ricotta if desired.

In the morning: Chop your onion and store it in the refrigerator in a bowl covered with plastic wrap; assemble the nonperishable ingredients on the counter; set a pot of water on the stovetop.

PENNE *with* ROASTED TOMATOES *and* SPINACH

If spinach integrated into pasta will cause a revolt among certain diners at your table, then just serve it on the side (see Sautéed Spinach with Garlic, page 155). About the butter: I find that adding it helps the tomatoes cling to the pasta more easily—and, shockingly, makes it taste more luxurious—but if you want to skip the fat, go right ahead.

Time: 35 minutes

1 pint grape tomatoes
(or however many
you have)

1 small onion,
roughly chopped

4 tablespoons olive oil

salt and pepper to taste

shake of red pepper flakes
(just enough to give kids
a taste of heat without
overwhelming them)

leaves from 1 fresh
thyme sprig (optional)

1 pound penne pasta

1 16-ounce bag fresh
spinach or 1 large bunch
of spinach

2 tablespoons unsalted
butter

1 garlic clove, halved

grated zest of one lemon
(about ½ teaspoon)

½ cup freshly grated
Parmesan

▸ Preheat the oven to 350°F.

▸ Place the tomatoes and onions on a rimmed baking sheet lined with foil. Add 2 tablespoons of the olive oil, salt and pepper, the red pepper flakes, and the thyme and toss with a spoon. (Do this gently so you don't rip the foil.) Bake for 25 to 30 minutes, until the tomatoes look shriveled and brown but not burned.

▸ While the tomatoes are roasting, bring a large pot of water to a boil. Add the pasta and cook according to the package instructions, adding the spinach to the pot during the last 30 seconds of cooking. Drain the pasta and spinach together, reserving ¼ cup of the pasta water. Place the pasta pot back on the burner over low heat and add the butter and the remaining 2 tablespoons of olive oil. Swirl the garlic halves in the oil to quickly infuse flavor, then remove the garlic after 1 minute.

▸ Return the pasta and spinach to the pot, and toss them with the tomato-onion mixture, the lemon zest, and the Parm. If it's looking gloppy, add a little reserved pasta water to help distribute the cheese more evenly.

In the morning: Chop the onion and store it in the refrigerator in a bowl covered with plastic wrap; assemble the nonperishable ingredients on the counter; set a pot of water on the stovetop.

CHORIZO
and KALE FRITTATA

Chorizo is one of those ingredients that really earns its keep in a kitchen. It's so flavorful that you don't need to do much to spin it into dinner. Plus, of course, it freezes beautifully, so it can always be there when you need it.

Time: 30 minutes

6 ounces smoked chorizo sausage, sliced crosswise into rounds

1 tablespoon olive oil

2 tablespoons chopped onion or shallot

pinch of salt

Handful of fingerling potatoes, thinly sliced crosswise into rounds like thick potato chips (about ½ cup)

1 handful of washed and roughly chopped kale

5 eggs

⅓ cup shredded Manchego cheese (or Jack)

1 tablespoon chopped fresh herbs, such as parsley or chives

▸ Preheat the broiler.

▸ In a cast-iron (or other ovenproof) skillet, fry the chorizo over medium-high heat until brown and crispy on both sides, about 2 minutes per side. Remove the chorizo from the skillet.

▸ Add the olive oil and cook the onions with salt for about 1 minute.

▸ Push the onions to the side of the pan and add the potatoes in a single layer. Cook for about another 5 minutes, or until the potatoes are crispy and mostly cooked through. Turn down heat to medium, add the kale, and stir until the leaves wilt. Return the cooked chorizo to the skillet.

▸ In a small bowl, whisk together the eggs, cheese, and herbs. Pour the egg mixture into the pan and stir lightly to make sure the chorizo, kale, and potatoes are evenly distributed.

▸ Cook without stirring for about 2 minutes. When the eggs are mostly cooked around the edges, transfer to the broiler. Broil for 1 to 2 minutes, until the eggs are cooked and the top is slightly puffy and golden. Cut into pizzalike wedges and serve.

Suggested sides: Asparagus with Vinaigrette (page 160); Barley with Herbs and Scallions (page 159)
In the morning: Chop your onion and store it in the refrigerator in a bowl covered with plastic wrap; slice your potatoes and submerge them in a bowl of water to prevent browning.

PAN-FRIED WHOLE WHEAT PIZZAS

Once you discover this method for making pizza, you will never be tempted to order Domino's again. (It's so easy that sometimes I find myself making one for the girls' after-school snack.) If you can swing it, pretend you're the omelet guy at the hotel breakfast buffet and use two skillets to save time.

Time: 35 minutes

Makes 2 personal pan pizzas

olive oil, for frying and brushing

1 16-ounce ball whole wheat pizza dough, split into two 8-ounce balls (if you want to use homemade, see dinneralovestory.com/perfect-pizza-crust)

$2/3$ cup Homemade Marinara Sauce (page 65) or store-bought pizza sauce

1 8-ounce ball fresh mozzarella, thinly sliced

2 to 3 fresh basil leaves, shredded

▸ Preheat the broiler.

▸ Add 1 tablespoon olive oil to a medium cast-iron or ovenproof pan set over medium heat.

▸ Roll each pizza dough half into a circle the size of your cast-iron pan. (The crust that results will be on the Sicilian side—slightly cakey. Use less dough if you favor thin-and-crisp-style pizza crust.)

▸ Add 1 piece of the rolled-out dough to the pan (loosely cover the other piece of dough with plastic wrap or a clean kitchen towel). Cook for 2 to 3 minutes, until the dough is bubbly on top and brown underneath. Flip, and layer on half of the sauce and half of the mozzarella. (Feel free to adjust the sauce amount if you are particular about it.)

▸ Cook for about another 2 minutes, or until the bottom is cooked through, then slip the pan under the broiler for 2 to 3 minutes, until the cheese looks bubbly. Remove the pan from the broiler and top the pizza with half of the basil. Remove the pizza from the pan, and repeat with the remaining piece of dough and toppings.

Suggested sides: Sauteed Spinach with Garlic (page 155) or Buttered Peas with Mint (page 159) On the weekend: Make Homemade Marinara Sauce (page 64).

PAN-FRIED WHOLE WHEAT PIZZAS *with* HAM *and* LEEKS

Now that you've nailed basic pizza (see previous page), you can customize as you wish, adding leftover meatballs, pepperoni slices, thawed and squeezed frozen spinach, fresh ricotta cheese, chopped ham and pineapple, or whatever vegetables you have left in the fridge, sautéed and plopped on the melted cheese. You can also skip the sauce and just top with mozzarella, leeks, and country ham. Mind-blowing.

Time: 25 minutes

Makes 2 personal pan pizzas

2 slices of country ham (or 2 slices of good-quality smoky bacon), chopped

olive oil, for frying

1 16-ounce ball whole wheat pizza dough, split into 2 8-ounce balls

1 8-ounce ball fresh mozzarella, chopped into shreds

2 medium-size leeks, washed, trimmed, finely chopped, and tossed in 1 tablespoon olive oil

handful fresh basil, shredded

▸ Preheat the broiler.

▸ Heat a medium cast-iron pan over medium heat. Add the ham and cook until crispy, about 2 minutes. Remove the ham and set aside; add a dash of olive oil to the pan.

▸ Roll each pizza dough half into a circle the size of your cast-iron pan. (The crust that results will be on the Sicilian side—slightly cakey. Use less dough if you favor thin-and-crisp-style pizza crust.)

▸ Add 1 piece of the rolled-out dough to the pan (loosely cover the other piece of dough with plastic wrap or a clean kitchen towel). Cook for 2 to 3 minutes, until the dough is bubbly on top and brown underneath. Flip, and layer on half of the mozzarella, half of the leeks, and half of the ham.

▸ Cook for another 2 minutes, or until the bottom has cooked slightly, then slip the pan under the broiler for 2 to 3 minutes, until the cheese looks bubbly and the leeks slightly toasted. Remove the pan from the broiler and top the pizza with half the basil. Remove the pizza from the pan, and repeat with the remaining piece of dough and toppings.

Suggested side: Quick Creamed Spinach (page 158) or Confetti Kale with Pecorino (page 161)

HOISIN TURKEY BURGERS

This is a natural next step for a burger-loving kid. If you replace the ground turkey or chicken with ground pork or beef (in Andy's words), "It's not like it's going to be bad." Hoisin is available in better supermarkets and Asian specialty stores.

Time: 30 minutes

1¼ pounds ground
turkey or chicken

2 scallions
(white and light green
parts only), minced
(about 1 tablespoon)

1 tablespoon peeled,
minced fresh ginger

1 tablespoon finely
chopped fresh cilantro

2 tablespoons
hoisin sauce, plus more
for serving

juice of ½ lime

¼ teaspoon cayenne
pepper

1½ teaspoons Chinese
five-spice powder

salt and pepper to taste

4 hamburger buns

hot mustard, for serving

▸ Preheat a grill or grill pan to medium-high.

▸ In a large bowl, combine the turkey, scallions, ginger, cilantro, hoisin, lime juice, cayenne, five-spice powder, and salt and pepper. Shape the turkey mixture into 4 patties, and grill over hot coals or in a grill pan, flipping frequently, for a total of 10 to 12 minutes, until the burgers are firm but not rock hard. (Alternatively, you can broil the burgers for 10 to 12 minutes on high.) Serve on buns with extra hoisin sauce or mustard as a condiment.

Suggested sides: Green Beans with Ginger and Garlic (page 159); Confetti Kale with Pecorino (page 161)
In the morning: Transfer your ground meat to the fridge to thaw if it's in the freezer.
On the weekend: Make the patties and freeze in ziplock bags for later use. Transfer the patties to the refrigerator in the morning so they'll be thawed for dinnertime.

CHICKEN *with* ARTICHOKES *in* CREAMY MUSTARD SAUCE

I love a good skillet dinner.
If you think the artichokes might be a deal breaker
with the kids—make it anyway!
(Isn't that what this month is about?!) Serve with
a baguette to sop up the juices.

Time: 30 minutes

$1\frac{1}{3}$ pounds chicken thighs (bone-in or boneless), salted and peppered

3 tablespoons olive oil

$\frac{1}{4}$ to $\frac{1}{2}$ teaspoon red pepper flakes

1 small onion, chopped (about $\frac{1}{2}$ cup)

8 ounces (about $1\frac{1}{2}$ cups) thawed frozen or canned artichoke hearts, drained and sliced lengthwise

grated zest of 1 lemon (about $\frac{1}{2}$ teaspoon)

1 teaspoon dried oregano

salt and pepper to taste

$\frac{1}{2}$ cup chopped grape tomatoes (or $\frac{1}{2}$ cup canned diced tomatoes), or to taste

$\frac{1}{2}$ cup white wine

$\frac{1}{2}$ cup chicken broth

$\frac{1}{3}$ cup heavy cream

2 teaspoons Dijon mustard

chopped fresh parsley or thyme leaves

▸ In a large nonreactive skillet, brown the chicken pieces in the olive oil over medium-high heat, in batches if necessary, 2 to 3 minutes per side. (They do not have to cook through.) Remove the chicken, reduce the heat to medium, and add the red pepper flakes and the onions. Cook for a minute or two, using a wooden spoon to scrape up any brown bits left over from the chicken. (Keep those brown bits in the pan—they add lots of flavor.) Add the artichoke hearts, lemon zest, oregano, and salt and black pepper. Cook for another 2 to 3 minutes then stir in tomatoes. Nestle the chicken thighs among the vegetables, then add the wine and chicken broth. Bring to a boil, then reduce to a simmer and cover. Cook for another 8 to 10 minutes, until the vegetables are tender and the chicken is cooked through.

▸ While the chicken mixture is simmering, in a small bowl whisk together the cream and mustard. Remove the skillet from the heat and stir in the creamy mustard sauce. Serve topped with parsley or thyme.

In the morning: Transfer your chicken to the fridge to thaw if it's in the freezer; chop your onion and store it in the refrigerator in a bowl covered with plastic wrap; assemble the nonperishable ingredients on the counter. Suggested side: Baguette or whole wheat flatbread

BAKED POTATO BAR

The best thing about this dinner?
You can get it started during your commute home.
If your kids are old enough, teach them how
to turn the oven to 450°F and put the potatoes
in before the oven gets hot.

Time: 60 minutes, including 45 to 60 minutes baking time

6 baking potatoes (or 1½ potatoes per diner)

6 pieces good-quality bacon, cooked

4 ounces cheese, such as Cheddar, feta, or Parmesan

1 head of broccoli, cut into florets and steamed

1 6-ounce bag fresh spinach, sautéed in olive oil with garlic (or in a little bacon fat after the bacon has been cooked)

2 large onions, sliced and cooked in olive oil on low heat for 15 to 20 minutes, until caramelized

sour cream

unsalted butter

ketchup

▸ Preheat the oven to 450°F.

▸ Put the potatoes in the oven and bake for 45 minutes to an hour, depending on the size of the potatoes.

▸ While the potatoes are baking, prepare the desired toppings.

▸ Remove the potatoes from the oven, split them open and top with the desired cheese. Broil them until the cheese is melted, then top with the desired add-ons. Try to make the vegetables nonnegotiable.

In the morning or on the weekend: Usually I prepare the toppings while the potatoes bake, but you can cook the bacon and onions, and steam the vegetables on the weekend or in the morning as well.

PASTA *with* PEAS, BACON, *and* RICOTTA

This recipe comes from Melanie Rehak, who is a former restaurant professional, the author of the cookbook Eating for Beginners, *a contributor to* Dinner: A Love Story, *and the mother of a onetime picky eater. But don't let all that scare you. Her recipe, though probably not endorsed by many cardiologists, is a cinch.*

Time: 25 minutes

1 pound tubular pasta
(such as rigatoni
or penne, which let
you trap the peas and
bacon bits better)

3 to 4 tablespoons
fresh ricotta cheese

½ pound bacon,
as lean as possible

¼ onion, chopped

1 10-ounce package
frozen peas

salt to taste

⅓ cup freshly grated
Parmesan, plus extra
for the table

freshly ground black
pepper

▸ Cook the pasta in salted boiling water. Add the ricotta to the bowl the pasta will be tossed in, and break it up with a fork if necessary. Drain the pasta and place in the bowl, tossing it immediately with the ricotta.

▸ Fry the bacon until crisp, drain it on paper towels, let it cool, then chop it up and set aside. While the bacon is cooling, pour off all but about 2 tablespoons of the bacon fat from the pan. Add the onions and the frozen peas to the pan (no need to thaw first). Cook over medium heat for 4 to 5 minutes (slightly less if thawed), stirring to thaw and coat the peas thoroughly.

▸ Add the chopped bacon back to the pan with the peas and onions, rapidly warm it all up, and pour the entire contents of the pan onto the pasta. Toss thoroughly, add the grated Parmesan and 2 or 3 grindings of pepper, toss again, and serve. Pass extra Parmesan at the table.

In the morning: Cook your bacon and store it in the refrigerator; set a pot of water on the stovetop.

GRILLED CHICKEN
with PEANUT CURRY SAUCE

*This was a big hit during my own Operation 30 Days—
mostly, I'd say, because my girls were thrilled by the concept of
chicken on a stick. If you don't have time to thread the
chicken on skewers, just skip that step, throw the chicken right
on the grill, and follow the same instructions from there.*

Time: 60 minutes

Special equipment:
1 package skewers (soaked
for 10 minutes if wooden)

CHICKEN

1 15-ounce can
unsweetened coconut milk

1 tablespoon low-sodium
soy sauce

1½ teaspoons curry
powder

juice of ½ lime

black pepper

1½ pounds boneless,
skinless chicken breasts
(4 medium breasts),
pounded and cut into
½-inch-thick pieces

PEANUT CURRY SAUCE

1 1-inch piece fresh
ginger, peeled

1 small garlic clove

½ cup creamy
peanut butter

2 tablespoons
low-sodium soy sauce

juice of ½ lime

1 teaspoon light brown
sugar, lightly packed

¼ to ½ teaspoon red
pepper flakes

⅓ cup water

handful of fresh
cilantro leaves,
chopped, for garnish

▶ Prepare the chicken: In a large bowl, whisk together the coconut milk, soy sauce, curry powder, lime juice, and black pepper until well combined. Add the chicken slices to the coconut-curry mixture, stirring to coat. Marinate, covered and refrigerated, for at least 30 minutes and up to 8 hours.

▶ Make the peanut curry sauce: With the motor running, drop the ginger and garlic clove into a blender or the bowl of a mini food processor and blend until finely chopped. Add the remaining sauce ingredients (except the cilantro) with ⅓ cup water and whirl until it reaches the desired consistency.

▶ Heat a stovetop cast-iron grill or grill pan (or build a medium fire in a charcoal grill). While it's heating, thread the chicken strips onto skewers, scraping off excess marinade as you work. Lightly oil the grill and cook the chicken, turning once, until cooked through, 3 to 4 minutes per side. Serve with the dipping sauce, and sprinkle everything with the cilantro.

Suggested side: Dilly Cucumber Salad (page 161), Rice with Cilantro and Lime (page 162)
In the morning: Pound, slice, and marinate the chicken; soak the wooden skewers for
10 minutes if using.
On the weekend: Make the peanut curry sauce and store it, covered, in the refrigerator.

SLOPPY JOES

*Here's a great 2.0 for the kid who is a big fan of chili.
It makes enough for four big sandwiches (or six mini "sliders").
My friend Jennie calls it a "Trojan horse" dinner,
since she hides chopped zucchini and carrots in the meat when
making them for her unsuspecting sons.*

Time: 25 minutes

3 tablespoons olive oil

½ onion, chopped

1 garlic clove, minced

1 pound ground turkey

½ can tomato paste

1 tablespoon chili powder

1 teaspoon dried oregano

pinch of ground cinnamon

salt and pepper to taste

4 burger buns or 6 small ciabatta rolls (or preferably something sturdy that won't fall apart under all the sauce)

4 to 6 slices sharp Cheddar cheese

sour cream (optional)

▶ In a large skillet set over medium heat, add the olive oil, onions, and garlic. Cook until soft, about 3 minutes. Add the turkey and cook until most of the pink is gone. (Here I usually drain the fat before proceeding.) Add the tomato paste, chili powder, oregano, cinnamon, and salt and pepper, and stir everything together. If it looks dry, add a little water. Reduce the heat and simmer for about another 5 to 10 minutes, until meat is cooked through and the flavors have melded.

▶ Meanwhile, preheat the broiler.

▶ When the turkey mixture is finished, heap a spoonful onto one side of a roll and top with a slice of Cheddar. Broil for 2 minutes, or until the cheese is melted. Top with sour cream, if desired, and the other bun half.

Suggested sides: Sweet potato fries; Halved Avocado with Vinaigrette (page 156); Roasted Cauliflower and Broccoli (page 161)

On the weekend: Make sloppy joe mixture, allow it to cool, and freeze it in a flattened ziplock.

In the morning: Transfer your ground meat to the fridge to thaw if it's in the freezer; chop your onion and store it in the refrigerator in a bowl covered with plastic wrap; set all the nonperishable ingredients on the counter.

SPAGHETTI *with* SHALLOTS *and* BRUSSELS SPROUTS

When I was a kid, I was as likely to try a Brussels sprout as I was to lend my sister my brand–new Benetton sweatshirt. (Most likely because fresh Brussels sprouts weren't as widely available back in the '80s.) Meanwhile, today my kids think Brussels sprouts, which we first sold to them as "baby cabbages," are about as common as baby carrots.

Time: 25 minutes

1 pound spaghetti
(or any ribbon pasta)

2 tablespoons olive oil

1 small shallot, chopped
(or a handful of
chopped onion)

shake of red pepper
flakes

2 to 3 large handfuls
(2 cups) of Brussels
sprouts, trimmed
and shredded
(buy preshredded
if you can; if you can't,
shred them as finely
as possible)

grated zest of ½ lemon

2 tablespoons cider or
red wine vinegar

salt and pepper to taste

½ cup freshly grated
Parmesan

▶ Cook the pasta according to the package directions. Reserve ½ cup of the cooking water, then drain the pasta.
▶ Meanwhile, heat the olive oil in a large, heavy skillet over medium heat. Add the shallots and red pepper flakes and sauté until the shallots have softened, about 2 minutes. Add the Brussels sprouts, lemon zest, vinegar, a little salt, and a twist of black pepper, then cook over medium-high heat until the Brussels sprouts are tender and lightly browned, about 4 minutes.
▶ Add the drained pasta to the Brussels sprouts along with the Parmesan, tossing to combine. Add pasta water as needed to loosen the mixture and distribute the cheese.

In the morning: Shred the Brussels sprouts if they're not already shredded, and store them in the refrigerator in a bowl covered in plastic wrap; chop the shallot or onion and store it covered in the refrigerator as well; assemble the nonperishable ingredients on the counter; set a pot of water on the stovetop.

CREAMY GREEK
CHICKEN NOODLE SOUP

Something creamy and magical happens to this soup when you whisk the eggs into the chicken broth. The technique can be somewhat exacting, so follow the instructions precisely or you might wind up with scrambled eggs. Once you nail that part, though, you won't believe how often you'll fall back on this for dinner.

Time: 25 minutes

2 tablespoons olive oil

¼ cup finely chopped carrots

¼ cup finely chopped onion

salt and pepper to taste

4 cups chicken broth

1 cup uncooked egg noodles (I like the skinny kind)

2 eggs

2 tablespoons fresh lemon juice

handful of fresh dill, chopped

1 cup cooked chicken, shredded or chopped (see page 52 for instructions)

▸ In a large saucepan over medium heat, heat the olive oil. Add the carrots and onions, season with salt and pepper, and sauté about 2 minutes, until carrots are slightly softened. Add the chicken broth and bring to a boil.

▸ Add the noodles and boil until the vegetables are tender and the noodles are just about cooked, about 4 minutes. Season again with salt and pepper and reduce the heat to low; let simmer.

▸ In a medium, heat-proof bowl, whisk together the eggs and lemon juice until smooth. Slowly ladle about ½ cup of the hot broth into the egg-and-lemon mixture, whisking to combine.

▸ Remove the simmering broth from heat. (Very important.)

▸ Very slowly, drizzle the egg mixture back into the pot, whisking constantly for 2 full minutes. Add salt and pepper, the dill, and chicken if you are using, and serve.

Suggested side: Baguette or whole wheat flatbread
On the weekend: Cook the chicken breasts. (See page 41, "Unpack and Prep for the Week.") Or make an entire batch of the soup and freeze in flattened ziplock bags.

MISO-GLAZED SALMON

White miso, which you can find at Asian specialty stores or better supermarkets like Whole Foods, is a good ingredient to debut during your monthlong challenge. It's sweet, surprisingly kid-friendly, and keeps in the fridge for ages.

Time: 15 minutes

¼ cup white miso

1 tablespoon
low-sodium soy sauce

3 tablespoons pure
maple syrup

½ teaspoon chile paste
or Sriracha

olive oil

1⅓-pound salmon fillet,
cut into four pieces

squeeze of fresh
lime juice

▶ Preheat the broiler.

▶ In a small bowl, whisk together the miso, soy sauce, maple syrup, and chile paste.

▶ Brush the salmon fillets with oil and place skin side down in a baking dish. Broil for 6 to 8 minutes, then remove the dish from the broiler. Slather the miso mixture on top of each fillet. Broil for another 2 minutes, or until the top turns golden and the fish is just cooked through. (Watch it carefully: The sugar in the glaze will burn.) Serve with a squeeze of lime juice.

Suggested sides: Green Beans with Ginger and Garlic (page 159); Sugar Snap Peas and Radish Salad (page 157).

In the morning: Mix together the miso glaze ingredients and store in the refrigerator covered with plastic wrap.

CHORIZO TACOS *with* SLAW *and* AVOCADO

*If the thought of firing up the blender or food processor on
a weeknight (or during morning prep) is laughable,
you can skip the sauce and just garnish your taco with cilantro,
lime, and yogurt or sour cream. This recipe makes enough
for two (killer) tacos per person.*

Time: 30 minutes

½ cup plain yogurt

⅔ cup cilantro

juice of ½ lime

¼ teaspoon ground cumin

salt to taste

10 to 12 ounces smoked chicken chorizo sausage, sliced crosswise into rounds

8 corn tortillas

1 cup shredded fresh spinach

¼ small napa cabbage, shredded (about 2 cups)

1 avocado, pitted, peeled, and sliced

▶ Using a blender or a mini food processor, blend together the yogurt, cilantro, lime juice, cumin, and salt. Set aside.

▶ In a large skillet (preferably cast-iron) over medium heat, fry the chorizo rounds until brown and crispy on both sides, about 2 minutes per side. Remove from the skillet to a paper-towel-lined plate.

▶ Raise the heat to medium-high and cook each tortilla until brown, about 30 seconds per side. Stack the tortillas on a plate under a clean kitchen towel to keep them warm until all are heated through.

▶ Top each tortilla with spinach, cabbage, chorizo rounds, avocado slices, and a heavy drizzle of the cilantro-yogurt dressing.

In the morning or on the weekend: **Make the dressing and store it, covered, in the refrigerator. Will keep for 7 to 10 days.**

CORNMEAL-CRUSTED FISH *with* HOMEMADE TARTAR SAUCE

Nothing warms the toddler heart quite like the golden crispy crust that results from dredging a piece of fish/chicken /shoe leather in flour, egg, and bread crumbs. But on nights when I just don't have the energy to set up the assembly line, I go with this slightly shorter technique.

Time: 25 minutes

TARTAR SAUCE

3 tablespoons mayonnaise

1 tablespoon chopped pickle

pinch of sugar

squeeze of fresh lemon juice

salt to taste

FISH

3 tablespoons olive oil, plus more as needed

½ cup cornmeal

1 teaspoon mustard powder

pinch of paprika

pepper to taste

1 pound freshest flounder fillets (or other mild white fish) you can find

½ cup milk, in measuring cup

▶ Make the tartar sauce: In a small bowl, combine the mayonnaise, chopped pickle, sugar, lemon juice, and salt. Set aside.

▶ Prepare the fish: Add the olive oil to a large skillet set over medium heat. On a dinner plate, mix together the cornmeal, mustard powder, paprika, and salt and pepper. Dip the flounder pieces into the cup of milk, dredge in the cornmeal mixture, then add to the hot pan. Cook for about 2 minutes per side, until the crust looks golden and crispy. Drain on paper towels. Repeat with the rest of the fish, adding more oil as necessary. Serve with the tartar sauce.

Suggested sides: Quick Creamed Spinach *(page 158); or* Buttered Peas with Mint *(page 159)*
In the morning: Make the tartar sauce. Store covered in the refrigerator.

CHICKEN BLTs

*We use chicken thighs here for a few reasons:
(1) they are tastier than their white-meat counterparts;
(2) they fit perfectly in a sandwich bun; and
(3) when you pan-fry thighs using this technique, it's
nearly impossible to under- or overcook them.*

Time: 30 minutes

4 slices of good-quality bacon

1 tablespoon olive oil

2 pounds boneless chicken thighs, seasoned with salt and pepper (about 4 to 6 thighs)

4 to 6 whole wheat burger buns

mayonnaise to taste

a few leaves of sturdy lettuce, such as romaine or Boston

2 ripe tomatoes, sliced

1 avocado, peeled, pitted, and sliced

▸ Set a large skillet over medium heat and add the bacon. Fry until crisp, about 4 minutes per side. Remove and drain on paper towels. Wipe a little of the bacon fat off the pan, then add the olive oil. Add the chicken to the skillet, skin side down, and cook for about 12 minutes, or until the skin is golden brown. Flip the chicken, then cook for about another 5 minutes, or until cooked through.

▸ Meanwhile, toast the buns. Spread the mayonnaise on the bun halves and layer on the bacon, lettuce, tomato, avocado, and chicken. (Add more than one piece of chicken for the adults if desired.)

Suggested sides: Corn with Butter and Cotija Cheese (page 157); sweet potato fries
In the morning: Transfer the chicken to the fridge to thaw if it's in the freezer. Cook the bacon and store, covered, in the refrigerator.

Note: Feel free to replace the regular mayo with Sriracha-spiked mayo. (See recipe on page 67.)

WHOLE WHEAT SPAGHETTI
with ROASTED CAULIFLOWER *and* BREAD CRUMBS

*Notice how I left the word anchovies out of the recipe title?
I did that because I don't want your kids (or you) to use it as an excuse
to skip over this one. I promise you won't taste any
fishiness—just that salty richness that upgrades the meal
to extra-special-weeknight status.*

Time: 30 minutes

1 head of cauliflower, florets only

6 tablespoons olive oil

salt and pepper to taste

shake of red pepper flakes (to taste)

1 pound whole wheat spaghetti

1 tablespoon unsalted butter

1 shallot, chopped

2 garlic cloves, minced

4 anchovies, minced

1 cup dried bread crumbs

Freshly grated Parmesan, for serving

▶ Preheat the oven to 400°F.

▶ On a rimmed baking sheet, toss the cauliflower in 3 tablespoons of the olive oil and season with salt, black pepper, and red pepper flakes. Roast for 20 to 25 minutes, or until the cauliflower is golden and crispy.

▶ Meanwhile, cook the spaghetti according to the package directions. Drain into a colander and toss with 1 tablespoon of the olive oil and the butter.

▶ Place the pasta pot back on the stove over medium-low heat and add the remaining 2 tablespoons of olive oil. Add the shallots, garlic, and anchovies. Cook for 2 minutes, or until the shallots and garlic are soft and the anchovies have broken down. Stir in the bread crumbs and cook until they are golden, about 5 minutes.

▶ Return the pasta to the pot, add the cauliflower, and toss everything together. Serve with freshly grated Parmesan.

Suggested side: Sautéed Spinach with Garlic (page 155)
In the morning: Chop the shallot and cauliflower; assemble the nonperishable ingredients on the counter; set a pot of water on the stovetop.

SPINACH
and FETA OMELET

Because my kids don't eat eggs—no matter how much I begged during our 30-day campaign—this recipe serves only one. I end up making it mostly on those nights when dinner gets derailed and only the grown-ups are eating. For a family of four, just make three (one for each adult, half for each kid), one after the other. Also: Use the freshest eggs you can get your hands on.

Time: 10 minutes

3 eggs

salt and pepper to taste

1 tablespoon olive oil

2 tablespoons
unsalted butter

1 garlic clove, halved

generous handful of
fresh spinach leaves,
washed and stemmed,
about 1½ cups (or ½ cup
thawed frozen spinach)

2 ounces feta cheese,
crumbled (about ¼ cup)

chives (optional)

▶ In a small bowl, whisk together the eggs, salt and pepper, and a dash of water. Add the olive oil and 1 tablespoon of the butter to a large cast-iron or nonstick skillet over medium heat. Swirl around the garlic halves and remove them before they brown. (This gives the oil a quick garlic infusion.)

▶ Add the spinach to the skillet and cook until slightly wilted, about 2 minutes. Using kitchen scissors, snip the spinach into small pieces while it wilts in the pan. Remove and set aside. Wipe down skillet.

▶ Melt the remaining tablespoon of butter in the skillet and add the egg mixture, tilting the pan to spread evenly. Cook for about 1 minute, then sprinkle the feta and cooked spinach down the center in a row. (The egg on top should still look a little runny.) Very gently, fold one third of the omelet over the filling, then fold the other side on top. Cook for another 1 to 2 minutes and slide onto a plate.

Suggested side: **Baguette toasts or whole wheat flatbread**

STEAK SANDWICHES
with **GRUYÈRE**

*We are big
"sandwiches for dinner" people—
especially when the thing
wedged between two pieces of bread
is a soy-marinated steak.*

Time: 35 minutes

1 pound skirt or top round steak (about 1 inch thick)

¼ cup low-sodium soy sauce

salt and pepper to taste

3 tablespoons olive oil

1 onion, sliced

1 tablespoon balsamic vinegar

1 garlic clove, halved

4 large slices of Gruyère or other Swiss cheese

1 baguette, sliced into 4 sandwich-size pieces and halved horizontally

pickles or cornichons or pickled jalapeños (optional)

▸ In a ziplock bag or shallow dish, toss the steak with the soy sauce and season with salt and pepper. Seal the bag or cover the dish and marinate the steak in the refrigerator for as long as you can, at least 15 minutes and up to 8 hours.

▸ In a large cast-iron skillet set over low heat, add 2 tablespoons of the olive oil and the onion slices and cook for 10 to 15 minutes, or until the onions have wilted and look slightly caramelized. Stir in the balsamic vinegar, turn up heat, and cook another minute. Remove onions from the pan into a bowl.

▸ Wipe the pan clean and add the remaining tablespoon of oil. Turn the heat to medium and add the garlic halves, swirling them to infuse the oil with garlic flavor. Remove the garlic. Blot the steak dry with paper towels. Raise the heat to medium-high and cook the steak until medium-rare, about 4 minutes per side. Let the steak rest for 5 minutes, then slice it on an angle into strips, about ¼ inch to ½ inch thick.

▸ Meanwhile, preheat the broiler. Add the cheese slices to the top baguette halves and broil until the cheese is melted, about 1 minute. (Broil the bottom halves at the same time; keep an eye on them so they don't burn.) Remove the baguettes from the oven and top with the steak, onions, and pickles, if using.

Suggested sides: Barley with Herbs and Scallions (page 159); White Beans and Spinach (page 156)
In the morning: Make the marinade and pour into a ziplock plastic bag over the sliced steak; chill in the refrigerator. Chop the onion and store separately, covered, in the refrigerator.

CHICKEN SAUSAGES
with **KALE SLAW**

This is a particularly good dinner for parents who are looking to leverage their kids' passion for hot dogs into something nutritious. The whole thing takes almost no time and is especially delicious when your summer grill is open for business.

Time: 30 minutes

1¼ to 1½ pounds good-quality chicken sausages

1 bunch of kale (preferably flat-leaf such as Lacinato/ Tuscan, which is more tender and less likely to cause a kid-led revolt), about 4 to 4½ cups

2 tablespoons olive oil

1 small shallot (or 3 to 4 scallions), chopped

squeeze of fresh lemon juice

salt and pepper to taste

¼ cup freshly shredded Parmesan or Pecorino

whole-grain mustard to taste

▸ In a skillet over medium heat (or on a grill over medium-hot coals), fry the sausages for 12 to 15 minutes, turning occasionally, until brown and cooked through.

▸ While the sausages are frying, slice the kale into shreds. In a large bowl, toss the kale with the olive oil, shallots, lemon juice, salt and pepper, and cheese.

▸ Serve the sausages and kale slaw with a dollop of whole-grain mustard.

*Suggested side: **Baked beans***
*In the morning or on the weekend: **Wash and shred your kale, then store in a ziplock bag in the refrigerator.***

There are so many great options for healthy chicken sausages. My favorites are chicken chorizo, sweet Italian, or chicken and apple sausage, any of which you can usually find in a good meat department or a great farmer's market.

SLOW-COOKER KOREAN SHORT RIBS

I know that many of my readers swear they would marry their Crock-Pots if they could, so I'd be remiss not to include at least one recipe for them in this chapter. One of my more generous readers, Anna Palubecki, sent this one to me, and it became an instant sensation on the blog. It's perfect on those mornings when you have forgotten to defrost—since the meat can go in frozen and still come out great.

**Time: 6 to 8 hours
(all hands-off time)**

3 to 4 pounds
country-style pork ribs
or beef short ribs
(again, meat can go
in frozen!)

1 cup light brown sugar,
packed

2 garlic cloves, smashed

1-inch piece ginger,
peeled and grated

1 cup low-sodium
soy sauce

3 fresh whole jalapeños

No slow cooker?
Go to dinneralovestory
.com/koreanshortribs for
stovetop instructions.

▸ Combine all of the ingredients in a slow cooker, stir in ½ cup water, and cook on low for 6 to 8 hours.

Suggested side: Green Beans with Toasted Almonds and Mint (page 155); Barley with Herbs and Scallions (page 159)

PULLED BARBECUE CHICKEN SANDWICHES

Wow, do I love these. There was a time in my life when you could open up my freezer and always find a bag of the juicy pulled chicken, just waiting to be thawed for dinner or for summer entertaining. Bonus points if you make it with Homemade Barbecue Sauce (see page 73).

Time: 35 minutes

1 tablespoon canola oil

1 small onion, finely chopped (about 1 cup)

2 garlic cloves, minced

1 cup Homemade Barbecue Sauce (page 73) or store-bought barbecue sauce

½ cup cider vinegar

1 bay leaf

1 chipotle pepper in adobo. (Don't add any adobo sauce, just a single saucy pepper. P.S.: They come in small cans and are easy to find in the Mexican section of most supermarkets.)

4 boneless, skinless chicken breasts (2¼ pounds), halved vertically if they are large, seasoned with salt and pepper

8 ciabatta rolls (or slider or sandwich rolls)

dill sandwich pickles or cornichons (optional)

Sandwich Slaw (page 162), optional

▸ In a large, heavy pot set over medium-low heat, add the canola oil and sauté the onions and garlic for 2 minutes. Add the barbecue sauce, cider vinegar, bay leaf, and chipotle pepper to the pot and whisk. Add the chicken and enough water to cover (1 to 1½ cups), whisking the water with the barbecue mixture until it's blended. Bring to a boil, then reduce the heat and simmer until the chicken is cooked through, 15 to 20 minutes.

▸ Remove the chicken from the pot and shred with two forks. Bring the sauce to a boil until it thickens and reduces, another 10 minutes. Once it's nice and thick, stir the chicken back in to coat well and heat through. Discard bay leaf, then heap chicken on the rolls.

▸ Serve the sandwiches with pickles or slaw if using.

Suggested side: Asparagus with Vinaigrette (page 160)
On the weekend: Make the pulled barbecue chicken and allow to cool completely. Spoon into ziplock bags, flattening slightly so they are easier to thaw under running water later on in the week. Reheat in a medium pot and assemble sandwiches as directed.
P.S.: You can freeze what remains of your can of chipotle peppers in adobo in a ziplock bag.

SUMMER STEW *with* CHICKEN, CORN, *and* SAUSAGE

*Summer and stew seem like strange bedfellows, but this recipe—
a version of which we first spied in* Gourmet *magazine in the late 1990s—is a
game-changer, and should probably only be made during peak corn and
tomato season. It's totally deconstructable, so if your kid just likes chicken or just
likes sausage, separate those out with some of the vegetables*

Time: 60 minutes

2 tablespoons olive oil, plus more if needed

3 links smoked chorizo or andouille sausage, sliced into coins

6 or 7 boneless chicken thighs, salted and peppered

½ medium onion, chopped

salt and pepper to taste

red pepper flakes to taste (optional)

2 to 3 cups fresh corn kernels

1 cup cherry or grape tomatoes, halved

chopped fresh basil leaves

▶ In a Dutch oven or large pot over medium heat, brown the sausage in the olive oil until crispy, about three minutes. Remove the sausage to a large plate and set aside. Raise the heat to medium-high and brown the chicken (in batches if necessary) on both sides until mostly cooked through, about twelve minutes total. Remove the chicken to the plate with the sausage. Turn down the heat to medium-low and add the onions, salt and pepper, red pepper flakes if using, and a little more oil if necessary. Stir until the onions are slightly wilted. Add the corn and tomatoes and stir until the vegetables release their juices.

▶ Nestle the chicken and sausage among the vegetables, cover, and simmer for another 5 to 10 minutes, until the chicken is cooked through. Sprinkle with the basil and serve in bowls, or separate into individual components for the kid who doesn't like things "mixed" and serve on a plate.

EASY HOMEMADE MACARONI *and* CHEESE

This one goes out to all those parents who are ready to break free from the tyranny of Annie's and Kraft. The great food writer Sam Sifton was the first to tell me to use milk instead of the traditional (time-consuming) bechamel. Revolutionary.

Time: 45 minutes

1 pound tubular
pasta, such as penne
rigate or rigatoni

1 tablespoon butter

1¼ cup grated Cheddar

1¼ cup grated Gruyère

½ cup grated Parmesan

¾ cups milk, warmed
in a saucepan or in
the microwave if possible

½ cup combination
of regular bread crumbs
or panko and crumbled
potato chips, mixed with
1 tablespoon olive oil

▸ Preheat the oven to 375°F. Prepare the pasta according to the package instructions and drain.

▸ Grease a medium-large baking dish with butter. In a large bowl, toss together the pasta and cheeses, reserving about ½ cup of cheese. Add pasta to the baking dish and pour milk all over.

▸ Sprinkle the top with bread crumbs, crumbled potato chips, and reserved cheese and bake for 20 to 25 minutes, until the casserole is golden on top and bubbly on the sides.

On the weekend: This will serve two adults and two kids with enough left over for one night of sides, so make it for Sunday dinner and save the remainder, covered, in the refrigerator.

Suggested sides: Sautéed Spinach with Garlic (page 155); or Curried Carrots (page 155)

CIOPPINO
(aka Tomato Fish Stew)

My friend Hugh Garvey, who used to write a great blog called Gastrokid, gets the credit for this one (meal number 15 in our 30-day trial). I'll never forget the sight of Phoebe inhaling the tomato broth like a milkshake. It was easy, with a deep flavor that you wouldn't expect with only a fifteen-minute simmer time.

Time: 30 minutes

2 tablespoons olive oil

2 large white fish fillets
(such as sole, flounder,
cod, or snapper),
salted and peppered
(and thawed if frozen)

2 garlic cloves, chopped

¼ cup white wine

1 12-ounce can whole
tomatoes, crushed by
hand (with juice)

salt and pepper to taste

A dozen assorted
shellfish such as mussels,
clams, or shrimp
(optional)

chopped fresh parsley,
for garnish

▸ In a medium saucepan, heat the olive oil over medium-high heat until smoking. Add the fillets and sauté for a few minutes to give them some golden color. Once the fillets are just about cooked through, remove them and set aside.

▸ In the same saucepan, reduce the heat to medium and sauté the garlic until fragrant but not brown. Pour in the white wine to deglaze the pan and stop the garlic from browning, then throw in the tomatoes with their juice. Reduce the heat to medium and let simmer, about 4 minutes.

▸ Add salt and pepper, then the reserved fish. If you have them, add the mussels, clams, or shrimp. Cover the pan and simmer until the mussels or clams open and/or the shrimp is cooked through, about 3 minutes. (Discard any mussels or clams that do not open.) Serve in shallow bowls, garnished with parsley.

Suggested side: **Baguette**

ZUCCHINI FRITTERS
with **SOUR CREAM** and **CHIVES**

You know the golden rule of feeding kids, right?
Turn anything into a pancake and they'll
eat it. This is especially useful when summer squash
is at its peak and you have more zucchini than
you know what to do with.

Time: 30 minutes

1½ pounds zucchini
(about 3 medium),
grated

salt

1 large egg, lightly beaten

¼ cup all-purpose flour

3 tablespoons
chopped scallions
(white and light
green parts)

3 tablespoons freshly
grated Parmesan

1 tablespoon cornstarch

pepper

⅓ cup vegetable oil

sour cream, for garnish

chopped fresh chives,
for garnish

▶ Place the zucchini in a colander set in the sink and toss with ½ teaspoon salt. Let stand for 10 minutes, then pat the zucchini thoroughly dry with a clean kitchen towel or paper towels, wrapping and wringing them if you have to. Place the zucchini in a large bowl and gently mix in the egg, flour, scallions, Parmesan, and cornstarch; season with salt and pepper.

▶ Heat the vegetable oil in a large skillet over medium heat. Working in batches, drop ¼-cup portions of the zucchini mixture into the oil, flattening slightly; cook until golden and crisp, about 3 minutes per side. Transfer the fritters to a paper-towel-lined plate. Serve topped with sour cream and chives.

In the morning or on the weekend: Grate the zucchini, drain, and store it in the refrigerator (for 2 to 3 days) in a ziplock bag or in a bowl covered with plastic wrap.

ASPARAGUS
and GOAT CHEESE TART

My kids are not likely to try something that includes eggs or goat cheese. Yours might be the same. So why is this recipe here? Because I once watched a six-year-old go crazy for something similar at a baby shower. So who am I to categorically write off a nice savory spring tart that can be made ahead and frozen?

Time: 1 hour

1 store-bought pie crust, pressed into a 9-inch pie dish

¾ cup milk

¾ cup half-and-half or heavy cream

3 eggs

pepper to taste

½ small onion, sliced

2 tablespoons olive oil

1 bunch of asparagus, trimmed of woody ends and chopped into 1-inch pieces

salt to taste

3 ounces goat cheese, crumbled

▶ Preheat the oven to 375°F.

▶ Prick the bottom of your pie crust all over with a fork and bake it for 8 minutes. While it's baking, in a medium bowl whisk together the milk, half-and-half, eggs, and some pepper.

▶ In a small skillet over low heat, sauté the onions in olive oil for 5 minutes, then add asparagus and cook another minute. Add salt and pepper. Remove from the heat and let cool.

▶ Remove the pie crust from the oven, then pour in the egg mixture. Add the asparagus-onion mixture, stirring gently to distribute. Sprinkle the goat cheese evenly on top. Bake for 35 to 40 minutes, until a knife inserted into the center comes out clean. If the top hasn't turned that appealing golden brown color, broil for a minute at the very end, watching carefully to make sure it doesn't burn.

Suggested side: Cucumber-Tomato-Parsley Salad (page 160)
On the weekend: Make the whole thing.
To freeze: Allow the tart to cool, then cover with foil and wrap in a freezer ziplock bag.
To reheat: Transfer to the fridge and thaw for at least 3 to 4 hours. Reheat in the oven (still covered with foil) at 350°F for 20 minutes, or until the tip of a knife inserted in the center feels warm to the touch.
To reheat directly from the freezer: Place the tart in a cold oven (still covered) and bring the temperature to 350°F. (This lets the icy dish heat gradually, preventing a Pyrex explosion in your oven.) Once the temperature reaches 350°F, bake the tart for 60 to 70 minutes, or until the tip of a knife inserted in the center feels warm to the touch.

CHICKEN PARM
MEATBALLS

*One of the most popular recipes I've ever run on the blog,
this was the result of Phoebe's begging for meatballs
and Abby's begging for chicken parm. (King Solomon would
be proud.) P.S.: If you get in the habit of making
(and freezing) these on Sunday, you won't be sorry.*

Time: 40 minutes

1¼ pounds ground chicken

½ cup dried bread crumbs

3 tablespoons finely chopped onion

2 tablespoons chopped fresh parsley

½ cup grated Parmesan (or Pecorino)

1 garlic clove, minced

1 teaspoon fennel seeds

1 egg, whisked

grated zest of ½ lemon

salt and pepper to taste

3 tablespoons olive oil

1 14-ounce can store-bought pizza sauce (such as Don Pepino's) or Homemade Marinara Sauce (page 64)

about 4 ounces fresh mozzarella (in thin slices; to pile on the cheese would be to cancel out the fact that you were virtuous enough to replace fatty beef with lean chicken)

▸ Preheat the oven to 400°F, setting a rack in the upper third of the oven.

▸ In a large bowl, use your hands to gently mix together the chicken, bread crumbs, onions, parsley, Parmesan, garlic, fennel seeds, egg, lemon zest, and salt and pepper. Shape into golf ball–size balls and place a few inches from each other on a lightly greased foil-lined rimmed baking sheet. In a small bowl, mix one spoonful of your pizza sauce with the olive oil. Brush this mixture on top of each meatball. Bake for 15 minutes.

▸ Remove the meatballs from the oven and turn on the broiler. Spoon some sauce on top of each meatball, and cover each with a slice of cheese. Broil for 3 to 5 minutes, until the cheese is bubbly and golden. Warm the remaining sauce in a small saucepan. Serve the meatballs with a dollop of sauce.

Suggested side: Sautéed Spinach with Garlic (page 155)
On the weekend: I like getting these in the oven right after a grocery shop. From start to finish, it'll take you about 25 minutes. After baking the meatballs, allow them to cool, then pop into a freezer bag.
To thaw: Transfer the frozen meatballs to the fridge in the morning so they're thawed by the time you get home. Preheat the oven to 350°F and bake the meatballs on a rimmed baking sheet for 15 minutes, then continue with the recipe as directed.

ROASTED SALMON
with LENTILS

The lentil salad part of this just gets better as the flavors meld in the refrigerator, so it's an ideal make-ahead meal. If your kids are going to be wary of all that insidious mixing of flavors—not to mention the lentils themselves— serve the lentils on the side.

Time: 30 minutes

1 cup lentils
(French lentils or those
pretty black belugas
if you can find them)

2½ to 3 cups any
combination of chicken
broth and water, or
enough to cover lentils
by about 1 inch

1½ teaspoons
Dijon mustard

¼ cup vinegar
(white or regular
balsamic, tarragon,
or red wine)

⅓ cup plus 1 tablespoon
olive oil

salt and pepper to taste

1 bunch of scallions
(white and light green
parts only), chopped

3 tablespoons
chopped bell pepper
(red or green)

leaves from 2 fresh
thyme sprigs
(or 1 tablespoon finely
chopped fresh parsley)

1¼-pound salmon fillet

▸ Preheat the oven to 400°F.

▸ In a medium pot, boil the lentils in the broth-water combo, then reduce the heat and simmer for 10 minutes (15 if you are using belugas). While the lentils are cooking, in a medium bowl make a vinaigrette by whisking together the mustard, vinegar, the ⅓ cup olive oil, and salt and pepper.

▸ When the lentils are tender but still hold their shape, drain them in a fine-mesh strainer. Toss the lentils in the bowl with the vinaigrette, adding the scallions, bell pepper, and thyme.

▸ Meanwhile, brush the salmon fillet with the remaining tablespoon of olive oil, season with salt and pepper, and roast for 10 to 15 minutes, until flaky. Break the salmon into bite-size pieces and toss with the lentils.

On the weekend: The entire lentil salad part of this dish can be made ahead of time, which means the only thing standing in the way of you and dinner is roasting the salmon at 400°F for 10 to 15 minutes.

In the morning: If you don't have time to make the lentil salad ahead of time, just prepare the vinaigrette in the morning before heading out.

KALE COBB SALAD

I love the kale twist on this classic, but no matter what greens you go with, you'll appreciate how deconstructable the meal is for kids. Note: It comes together really fast if you've prepped the chicken ahead of time.

**Time: 30 minutes
(45 if you aren't starting
with cooked chicken)**

2 eggs

2 cooked bone-in split
chicken breasts or
2 whole boneless breasts
(see page 52 for
instructions)

1 large bunch of kale,
shredded

3 pieces of bacon or ham,
cooked and chopped
into small pieces

2 tablespoons minced
scallions (white and
light green parts only),
red onion, or shallot

½ cup chopped tomatoes

½ cup crumbled blue
or feta cheese

1 avocado, peeled, pitted,
and chopped

your favorite dressing
(or see Basic Vinaigrette,
page 51)

▶ Place the eggs in a small pot and cover with water. Bring to a boil, then immediately cover and remove the pot from the heat. Remove the eggs after 14 minutes and allow them to cool before peeling. Chop into pieces.

▶ In a large, flat bowl or on a platter, arrange the chicken, eggs, kale, bacon, scallions, tomatoes, cheese, and avocado in rows, salad-bar style, so your kids can pick what they'd like and leave what they don't. Have each diner toss (or not toss) his or her own salad with dressing at the table.

On the weekend: Hard-boil your eggs, roast the chicken, and make the vinaigrette. Store each ingredient separately in the refrigerator.

In the morning: Make the vinaigrette, cook the bacon, and store each separately in the refrigerator.

CRISPY RICE OMELET

*If you fall off the wagon this
month and order your fair share of
Chinese takeout, don't despair.
Take any leftover rice and make
a few of these.*

Time: 15 minutes

1 tablespoon canola oil

2 tablespoons minced scallions (white and light green parts only) or onions

½ teaspoon peeled, minced fresh ginger

1 small garlic clove, minced

shake of red pepper flakes, or to taste

1½ cups leftover rice, preferably sticky Chinese takeout

4 eggs

2 teaspoons low-sodium soy sauce, plus more for serving

1 cup frozen peas, or to taste

▸ Preheat the broiler.

▸ Add the canola oil to a 10-inch cast-iron or nonstick skillet set over medium heat. Add the scallions, ginger, garlic, and red pepper flakes and cook for about 1 minute until everything is soft and fragrant.

▸ Add the rice and spread it out in one layer, raising the heat a bit. Don't stir for about a minute so the rice gets nice and crispy. Stir again and wait another minute. Meanwhile, in a medium bowl whisk together the eggs and soy sauce and add the peas. Reduce the heat to medium-low and pour the egg mixture over the fried rice, tipping the pan so the egg distributes itself evenly over the rice.

▸ Cook until the underside is crispy, 4 to 5 minutes. Transfer to the broiler and broil for 3 minutes, or until the egg looks golden and bubbly on top. Serve in wedges with a drizzle of soy sauce.

Suggested sides: Halved Avocado with Vinaigrette (page 156); Tomatoes with Feta and Balsamic (page 157)
On the weekend: Make the rice, if you're not going to use takeout, and store it in the refrigerator.
In the morning: Assemble the nonperishable ingredients on the counter.

GREENS *with* CHICKEN, CHERRIES, BLUE CHEESE, *and* CANDIED WALNUTS

I ate something like this at a beachside café in South Carolina, and I replicate it in my kitchen whenever I just can't face the idea of cooking. I always buy the candied walnuts instead of making them myself, but if you're inclined to do a homemade version, go for it.

**Time: 10 minutes
(45 if you don't start
with cooked chicken)**

3 medium-size cooked
chicken breasts, sliced
(see note on page 52)

3 to 4 generous handfuls
of fresh greens, such
as mesclun, romaine,
arugula, or a mix

¼ to ½ cup tart dried
cherries (such as
Montmorency cherries
from Trader Joe's)

½ cup crumbled blue
cheese (or to taste)

⅔ cup candied walnuts
(store-bought, or
homemade if you're man
enough. I'm not.)

snipped fresh chives
(or chopped scallions,
white and light green
parts only)

homemade vinaigrette
(see page 51)

▶ In a large serving bowl, toss all of the ingredients.

*Suggested sides: Whole wheat flatbread; Barley with
Herbs and Scallions (page 159)*
*On the weekend: Make a vinaigrette (page 51) and store
in the refrigerator. Cook the chicken.*

CHICKEN CHILI

Some version of this is always in our freezer, loyally waiting to be called on for dinner duty. Serve with toppings such as avocado chunks, shredded Cheddar cheese, sour cream, and chopped cilantro.

Time: 45 minutes

1 onion, chopped

1 garlic clove, minced

3 tablespoons olive oil

1 pound ground chicken, or chicken breasts cut into ½-inch pieces

salt and pepper to taste

4 tablespoons chili powder

1 28-ounce can diced tomatoes (with juice)

1 teaspoon dried oregano

¼ to ½ teaspoon cayenne pepper

1 bay leaf

¼ teaspoon ground cinnamon

1 14-ounce can white beans, rinsed and drained

▶ In a Dutch oven or other heavy-bottomed pan, over medium-low heat, sauté the onions and garlic in the olive oil for about 3 minutes. Raise the heat to medium-high and brown the chicken for about 5 minutes, until it loses its pink color. Add salt and pepper and the chili powder—get it sizzly so the seasonings start cooking—then add the tomatoes and the oregano, cayenne, bay leaf, and cinnamon. Reduce the heat, simmer for 10 to 15 minutes, and add the beans. Cook for another 5 minutes, or until the beans are warmed through. Discard the bay leaf.

Suggested sides: Tomato and Avocado Salad (page 156); Confetti Kale with Pecorino (page 161) On the weekend: Cook and cool the chili; store, covered, in the refrigerator for up to 3 days, or freeze in flattened ziplock freezer bags. To thaw: Transfer from the freezer to the fridge in the morning. If it's still frozen come dinnertime, run the sealed bag under cold water until it softens. Remove the chili from the plastic bag and add to a pot with a little water. Heat on low, covered, until warmed through.

MAPLE CANDY PORK CHOPS

My friend Rory coined the name
when she was serving these to her three-year-old.
Her rule: Whenever a dish is remotely sweet—
and thanks to the maple syrup marinade, this one is—
use the word candy *in the name. Instant hit.*

**Time: 25 minutes
(plus an hour's
marinating time)**

4 boneless center-cut
pork chops

⅓ cup pure maple syrup

3 tablespoons canola oil

¼ cup low-sodium
soy sauce

¼ cup rice wine vinegar

1 garlic clove, halved,
or a shake or two
of powdered garlic

▸ Place the pork chops in a ziplock bag. Add the maple syrup, canola oil, soy sauce, rice wine vinegar, and garlic. Marinate anywhere from 60 minutes to overnight.

▸ When ready to cook, preheat the oven to 450°F. Remove the chops from the marinade and pat dry with paper towels, scraping off any garlic that clings to the meat. Place the chops on a foil-lined rimmed baking sheet and bake, flipping once halfway through, for 15 to 20 minutes, until firm in the center but not rock hard.

Suggested sides: Beets with Feta and Chives (page 160); Corn with Butter and Cotija Cheese (page 157); sweet potato fries
In the morning: Marinate the pork chops and place in the refrigerator.

CHICKEN
and BARLEY SOUP

*As far as rich, hearty soups that fill a house
with happiness go, this one does the trick. Make your
life really easy: Whip it up on the weekend
and freeze it for use later in the week. Serve with
a fat slice of good bread.*

Time: 1 hour 10 minutes

2 tablespoons olive oil

½ teaspoon red pepper flakes

1 cup chopped yellow onion

1 cup peeled and chopped carrots (about 1 large carrot)

1 cup chopped celery (about 2 celery stalks)

½ cup chopped red bell pepper (about ½ bell pepper)

salt and pepper to taste

4 cups chicken broth, plus more as needed

1 bay leaf

4 fresh thyme sprigs

3 to 4 boneless chicken breast halves

½ cup uncooked barley

handful of chopped fresh parsley, for garnish

▸ In a large stockpot, warm the olive oil and red pepper flakes over medium heat for 1 to 2 minutes. Add the onions, carrots, celery, bell pepper, and salt and pepper and cook for 10 to 12 minutes, or until the onions are soft. Add the broth, bay leaf, and thyme and bring to a boil. Add the uncooked chicken and simmer, over medium-low heat, for 15 to 20 minutes.

▸ Remove the chicken from the pot and, using two forks, shred it. Return the chicken to the pot, add the barley, and simmer on low heat, covered, for 20 to 25 minutes, or until the barley is tender but not mushy. Add more broth, if necessary. Discard the bay leaf. Sprinkle with parsley and serve.

Suggested sides: Crackers, baguette, or whole wheat flatbread
On the weekend: Make and freeze the entire recipe!
To freeze: Allow the soup to cool, then ladle it into two or three ziplock freezer bags. Think about how you'll be using the soup. Will the whole family be eating it at the same time or will you want to dole it out in single portion sizes? That should determine the size and quantity of the bags you use. Lay the bags flat to freeze.
To reheat: Run your flattened bags under water. Squeeze the thawed soup into a saucepan and heat over low heat, adding enough water to thin it a bit without making it too brothy.

ASIAN SLAW *with* CHICKEN

*This dinner is in danger of becoming the only one
I make from June through September. It's so clean-tasting
and healthy and it comes together superfast if
you can have at least a few of the components ready
to go beforehand.*

**Time: 15 minutes
(60 minutes if you don't
start with cooked chicken)**

DRESSING

3 tablespoons rice
wine vinegar

1 teaspoon light brown
sugar, lightly packed

salt to taste

1 teaspoon fish sauce
(available at Asian
specialty stores and
better supermarkets)

juice of ½ lime
(about 1 tablespoon)

1 teaspoon peeled,
minced fresh ginger
(crucial)

1 drop hot sauce
or 1 teaspoon minced
jalapeño

⅓ cup neutral oil
such as grapeseed
or vegetable oil

SALAD

2 to 3 large handfuls
of shredded red cabbage
(½ medium head)

½ handful of shredded
baby spinach

½ cup shredded carrots

1 cup raw sugar
snap peas, trimmed
and chopped into
bite-size pieces

4 scallions (white and
light green parts only),
chopped

½ cup chopped fresh
cilantro leaves

handful of chopped
peanuts (optional)

shredded chicken from
2 split chicken breast
halves (see page 52)

▸ In a large serving bowl, whisk together the dressing ingredients. Add the salad ingredients and toss until combined. If you are afraid your kids won't touch it, separate out the elements you are sure they will like and reserve some dressing for them as a dip.

On the weekend: Make the dressing and store in the refrigerator. Cook the chicken: See instructions on page 52.

22
QUICK
SIDES

When a recipe does not feel like a complete meal to me—i.e., Cornmeal-Crusted Fish with Homemade Tartar Sauce (page 108)—I will always suggest serving it with one of the side dishes on the following pages that save my life on a daily basis. Whenever possible (this is hard in the colder months when the market pickin's are slim) try to pair cooked dishes with no-cook sides. It's always nice to have a hit of freshness on the plate. Also, I never, repeat NEVER, feel guilty about dumping a can of baked beans into a pot for a quick side dish. It's not homemade, no. But it isn't a big hulking piece of nutrient-free white bread or white rice, either, which was how I was wired to define "side dish" for so much of my childhood.

Sautéed Spinach with Garlic
Add 1 tablespoon olive oil to a large skillet. Swirl around
1 halved garlic clove, cut side down, to infuse the oil. Remove the
garlic clove. Add a shake of red pepper flakes and 12 ounces
of fresh spinach. Stir as the mound of leaves gradually wilts way
more than you ever think it will. Add a hefty pinch of salt and black
pepper. Snip the spinach leaves with kitchen scissors while still
in the skillet.

Curried Carrots
Peel 4 large carrots and cut into ¼-inch rounds. Toss them in a
pot with ½ cup water (or just enough to cover), 2 teaspoons curry
powder, a small pat of butter, some kosher salt, and a squeeze
of honey. Simmer, covered, for 15 minutes, or until tender.

Green Beans with Toasted Almonds and Mint
In a large frying pan, heat 2 tablespoons olive oil and 1 tablespoon
unsalted butter over medium heat. When the butter has melted,
add ¼ cup slivered almonds and cook for 2 minutes, or until they
darken slightly in color. Add 2 cups trimmed green beans and
cook for 2 minutes, stirring occasionally. Add a generous squeeze
of lemon juice and a few pinches of salt and remove to a platter.
Sprinkle with chopped fresh mint.

Tomato and Avocado Salad

Halve 1 avocado, remove the pit, peel, and cut into chunks. In a medium bowl, toss with about 1½ cups halved grape tomatoes, 3 chopped scallions (white and light green parts only), a generous drizzle of olive oil, salt and pepper, a spritz of lime juice, and chopped fresh cilantro to taste.

Halved Avocado with Vinaigrette

Halve 2 avocados and remove the pits. Pour salad dressing into each indentation left by the removed pit. Depending on what else is on the plate I like ginger-miso dressing or homemade vinaigrette (see Basic Vinaigrette, page 51). Easy and old-school. But not as old-school as Wishbone, which is how Andy ate this as a kid.

White Beans and Spinach

In a medium skillet, sauté a halved garlic clove, cut side down, in a few glugs of olive oil. Let it infuse the oil for a minute, then remove. Add 2 tablespoons chopped onions (or shallots or scallions—white and light green parts only) and a shake of red pepper flakes and cook until the onions are soft, about 2 minutes. Stir in 1 can of rinsed and drained white beans (such as Great Northerns or cannellini). Add a handful of thawed and well-squeezed frozen spinach, lightly mashing the beans and spinach together. Add salt and black pepper and stir. Serve with freshly grated Parmesan.

Sugar Snap Peas and Radish Salad
In a medium bowl, toss together 2 cups of the sweetest sugar snap peas you can find (trim off the ends if it's not too big of a pain); 1 radish, sliced into thin coins; ¼ cup chopped fresh mint; a squeeze of lime juice; sea salt; about 1 tablespoon chopped scallions (white and light green parts only); and a tiny drizzle of olive oil. This is best in the spring when the snap peas are peaking.

Tomatoes with Feta and Balsamic
If it's peak tomato season, you don't have to do anything at all to those tomatoes (except maybe add a little sea salt). But you can also cut them into thick slices (about 1 tomato per diner), then top with crumbled Greek feta, a light drizzle of good-quality balsamic vinegar (balsamic can be overpowering so always use sparingly), and a drizzle of olive oil.

Corn with Butter and Cotija Cheese (or Parmesan)
Boil shucked sweet corn for 5 minutes. Spread butter on the corn while the corn is still hot and sprinkle with cotija or Parmesan cheese. If it is peak corn season, forget the cheese and eat boiled corn on the cob with butter and salt only. Anything else is, obviously, blasphemy.

Quick Creamed Spinach

Thaw a box or bag of frozen spinach by placing it in a colander and running warm water over it for a few minutes. Press down on the spinach to squeeze out all the liquid. In a small frying pan over medium heat, add 1 tablespoon olive oil and $\frac{1}{4}$ small onion (chopped), salt, black pepper, and a few red pepper flakes (optional, as always). After 5 minutes, add the spinach and toss with the onions until the spinach is heated through. Sprinkle in 1 to 2 teaspoons flour and stir. Add $\frac{1}{3}$ to $\frac{1}{2}$ cup milk (nonfat, 1%, 2%, whole . . . any kind but chocolate!), depending on how creamy you like your creamed spinach, and a pinch of freshly ground nutmeg. Stir until heated through.

Whole Grains with Vegetables (Barley, Bulgur, Couscous)

This works with virtually any whole grain. I rely heavily on those packages of 10-minute parboiled barley and bulgur you can find at most supermarkets, but if you can't find them, just use whole wheat couscous, which only takes about 5 minutes to cook. Prepare according to the package instructions, then toss in any or all of the following: chopped tomatoes, chopped or torn mint, chopped scallions (white and light green parts only), chopped canned artichokes, salt and pepper, a tiny drizzle of good-quality balsamic vinegar, and a little olive oil. Garnish with crumbled feta. If you dig olives (I do not), I'm guessing they'd be good in there, too. (Note: I eat some version of this almost every weekday for lunch.)

Green Beans with Ginger and Garlic

Add 2 tablespoons olive oil to a large skillet set over medium heat, along with 2 teaspoons peeled, minced fresh ginger, 3 to 4 chopped scallions (white and light green parts only), a shake of red pepper flakes, and salt and black pepper. Cook until the ginger and scallions are soft and aromatic, about 1 minute. Add 3 cups trimmed green beans (or haricots verts) and 1 minced garlic clove. Cook, uncovered, until the green beans are tender but still crispy, about 4 minutes.

Barley with Herbs and Scallions

Prepare 1 cup barley according to the package directions (or refer to page 53). When finished, toss in 4 chopped scallions, ¼ cup olive oil, the juice of ½ lemon, and snipped herbs such as parsley, basil, or thyme.

Buttered Peas with Mint

In a large skillet, melt 2 to 3 tablespoons unsalted butter over medium heat. Add 1½ cups thawed frozen peas. (You can run them under warm water to accelerate the thawing process; just try to dry them as much as possible before proceeding.) Heat until warmed through. Remove from the heat and sprinkle with 2 tablespoons chopped fresh mint and salt to taste.

Beets with Feta and Chives
Whole Foods and Trader Joe's both sell cooked beets, which used to turn me off with their shrink-wrapped sliminess. But the truth is, there's hardly anything added to them and they're pretty tasty. I cut them in quarters, then drizzle olive oil on top and sprinkle with crumbled feta, snipped fresh chives, salt, and pepper. Also: There is no crime in substituting goat cheese for the feta. If you have time to use fresh beets, roast them wrapped in aluminum foil for 40 minutes at 425°F and peel.

Asparagus with Vinaigrette
Snap off the woody ends of the asparagus. Boil gently in a large, deep skillet for 2 to 4 minutes (2 for skinny stalks, 4 for thicker) and immediately plunge into ice water to stop the cooking (and to preserve the bright green color). Drizzle your favorite vinaigrette on top (see Basic Vinaigrette, page 51).

Cucumber-Tomato-Parsley Salad
In a medium bowl, whisk together $\frac{1}{3}$ cup olive oil, the juice of $\frac{1}{2}$ medium lemon, salt, pepper, and a handful of freshly chopped parsley. Peel 1 medium cucumber. Halve it lengthwise, then, using a spoon, scrape the seeds out of the middle, creating "canoes," as my kids call them. Chop into rough pieces and add to the bowl, along with $1\frac{1}{2}$ cups chopped grape tomatoes. Toss to combine.

Confetti Kale with Pecorino

In a salad bowl, whisk together ¼ cup red wine vinegar or apple cider vinegar, 2 teaspoons Dijon mustard, 1 teaspoon sugar, and ⅓ cup olive oil. Add 1 head of Lacinato (Tuscan) kale that's been stemmed and sliced into shreds. (Hence: confetti.) Add a handful of shredded Pecorino and toss. If you're feeling adventurous, throw in a handful of pomegranate seeds. (Pomegranates and kale pushing your luck? Replace the poms with avocado chunks.)

Dilly Cucumber Salad

In a medium bowl, whisk together ½ cup seasoned rice wine vinegar, ¼ cup finely chopped fresh dill, and salt and pepper to taste. Add 2 thinly sliced hothouse cucumbers (the kind that come shrink-wrapped) and toss to coat.

Roasted Cauliflower and Broccoli

Preheat the oven to 400°F. Separate 1 head of cauliflower and 1 head of broccoli into florets. On a rimmed baking sheet, toss the florets in olive oil to lightly coat. Season with a shake of red pepper flakes and salt and black pepper to taste. Spread out on the baking sheet and roast for 15 to 20 minutes, until the vegetables look crispy but not burnt. Squeeze fresh lemon juice over the vegetables and sprinkle with freshly grated Parmesan, if desired.

Sandwich Slaw

In a medium bowl, whisk together $\frac{1}{3}$ cup cider vinegar, 3 tablespoons mayonnaise, $\frac{1}{2}$ teaspoon celery seed, $1\frac{1}{2}$ teaspoons honey, a handful of chopped fresh cilantro or chopped dill (or a combo), salt, and pepper. Shred $\frac{1}{2}$ small head of green cabbage (about 5 cups) and toss with the dressing.

Rice with Cilantro and Lime

Prepare $1\frac{1}{2}$ cups short-grain white rice according to the package directions. When cooked, toss with $\frac{1}{2}$ cup chopped fresh cilantro, a heavy squeeze of lime juice, and salt to taste.

Cheater Specials

—

I stockpile these and never, ever feel guilty about working them into the rotation if I just can't get my act together to do every single thing from scratch.

- *Canned organic baked beans*
- *Canned black beans (simmered with a bay leaf and a squeeze of fresh lime juice)*
- *Baguettes—or, if you can find them, par-baked baguettes, which you toss into a 375°F oven and which, 15 minutes later, make your home smell like a Parisian bakery*
- *Frozen organic sweet potato fries (I like Alexia brand)*
- *Whole wheat flatbread, wrapped in foil and warmed in a 350°F oven*

KEEP-THE-SPARK-ALIVE DINNERS

You know that I will always have a special place in my heart for a simple, superfast, surefire weeknight meal. As I've made abundantly clear in this book—and in my tenure as a food blogger and parent—those are the kind of dinners you are going to be relying on most heavily throughout this 30-Day challenge. They will, in fact, probably be the dinner warhorses of your foreseeable future—if your foreseeable future includes family and children and family and . . . *living.*

But as important as these meals are, I'm convinced they alone will not convert a dinner infidel into a believer. They will get you through Operation 30 Days, yes. But another kind of meal is going to get you through Operation Lifetime Family Dinner. That's what I hope this chapter helps you with.

For a second here, I want you to think of your daily commute to work. The kind of commute when you have a nine o'clock meeting and the freeway is backed up. Or think about the after-school pinball-driving to ballet then soccer then back to ballet again. In other words, think about when your traveling is not at all about the journey. It is singularly about the destination—and getting to your destination as efficiently as possible. Maybe even with the right cleats, leotard, and hairbands on the right kids.

Now compare that kind of driving to the kind where you get in the car for a summer road trip and set off to explore a new town: Maybe you'll pull into a scenic overlook to take in a mountain view; or uncover a dilapidated seafood shack down a dune road that you just know by its hand-painted sign will be home to the best lobster rolls in New England; or maybe you'll find a great old bookstore—one with some vintage Donald

Duck comics—when all you were really searching for was a single espresso to power you through the rest of the afternoon.

Technically speaking, both of these scenarios can be slotted under the category of "driving," just as **preparing weeknight dinners** and weekend dinners both fall under the category of "cooking." But only the off-roading scenario has the power to remind you how freaking fantastic—how restorative—it can be to take your time, to open yourself up to exploration and discovery, to switch up the routine every now and then.

That is how I want you to think of the recipes on the following pages. If the goal of my Go-To Weeknight Meals is to get them to the table as fast as possible so that you can sit at the table unscathed, ready to listen to your children regale you with tales of who won wall ball (and, even more salacious, who cheated!), then the goal of the recipes in this section is to remind you that dinner is not just about eating. It's about the process of making dinner, a reminder that dinner doesn't only have to be a soulless slog; it can be enjoyable, and it can be savored. I'm convinced this is how you prevent falling out of love with cooking when kids come along—how you *keep the spark alive.*

I'll never forget my first Keep-the-Spark-Alive dinner. It was March 3, 2002, a date that is seared in memory not just because it's written right there in my dinner diary, but because it was the **first meal** Andy and I cooked together after Phoebe was born. We were in that new-baby timewarp mode—napping and nursing, nursing and napping, wondering why the baby wouldn't go to sleep when we turned off the light, like normal people did. When my visiting mother-in-law, Emily, wasn't cooking hot dinners for us, our meals mostly consisted of standing in front of the refrigerator with a fork Ψ, grabbing bites out of foil-wrapped casseroles and lasagnas that had been delivered to us by well-wishing friends. Shortly after Emily left, and our casserole supply had been officially depleted, Andy and I found ourselves in the kitchen alone. We had just put Phoebe down for the night (or, more likely, for an hour or two) and asked a question that almost seemed like it was from another life:

"What should we do for dinner?"

We could've ordered takeout—we lived in Brooklyn, where Middle Eastern or Thai or Chinese or West Indian or Italian or Bangladeshi food could've been at our doorstep in mere minutes—but we felt like eating homemade food. (And we felt like cooking.) There were some chicken pieces in the fridge and tons of gift-wrapped wine (the best baby gift of all), and before long we were back into the routine, short-cutting one of our favorite midwinter dinners: Julia Child's signature coq au vin. Because newborn Phoebe's sleeping was still erratic, we knew **we didn't have time** for the real-deal version, which called for two hours of simmering, among other tasks we didn't think our tired brains could handle, so we took some liberties. We used chicken thighs instead of hacking up a whole chicken. We skipped the igniting of the cognac (and the cognac itself). Instead of making separate recipes for brown-braised onions and sautéed mushrooms, as Julia instructs, we just threw both into the pot with the chicken. We put Ryan Adams's new album in the CD player (on low, so we could still hear the baby monitor); **we sipped some of the Pinot** that had gone into the pot. ━🥣 We plotted my maternity leave and talked about what a genius our two-week-old was. And even though the whole thing—from the chopping to the bowl-licking—took an hour and a half, it was the first chunk of time we'd had to ourselves since Phoebe had been born. **And, I have to say, it felt really good.**

It was right then that I began to develop a theory about parenting. Yes, it basically robbed me of my free time, but it also forced me to figure out what was important enough to do in the little free time I had. Of all things, stewing chicken with wine, while operating on less than four hours of sleep, was the first thing to make the cut.

I like to think dinner has been something of a ♥ love story for me because it's always been so much bigger than the fifteen minutes sitting at the table. **I crave the buildup to dinner.** I need to be sipping a nice Sangiovese and catching up with Andy or friends. Or I need one kid tackling decimals at the kitchen table, or sitting Indian-style on the counter snacking on chips and salsa, or in the adjoining room screeching her way through something on the cello. I need the aromas of sautéed onions and browning steaks swirling about the house the way smells do in Bugs Bunny, pulling family members into the kitchen in a state of weakened hypnosis. Maybe it's because I'm a writer, but I need the narrative arc of dinner. That way, even if my kid wrinkles her nose (again) at the sweet and spicy tofu (see page 198), it never feels like the entire evening is a washout.

So how can you identify the kind of meals that remind you how much **you love to cook?** What are the official hallmarks of a Keep-the-Spark-Alive dinner? Well, identifying one can be a slippery science, but the meal might possess any one of the following characteristics:

- **The meal might take a little longer to put together, forcing you to slow down and savor the process.**
- It might require a trip to the farmer's market to see what's fresh instead of only a trip to the supermarket to see what's on sale.
- **It might require help from the kids—i.e., a "project dinner."**
- It might be the kind of dinner you usually buy in the store and want to try making yourself. (Ravioli, page 176! Tempura, page 178!)
- **It might require using an ingredient you wouldn't have ever thought your kid would go for. (For us, that's tofu; for you it might be anything from chicken to sushi.)**
- Or it might require an ingredient or technique that you've been meaning to explore for, oh, about the same number years as there are candles on your oldest's birthday cake.

I have suggested fourteen recipes here that might provide the shot of inspiration you are hungry for, but you should, of course, feel free to supplement with the recipes you've dog-eared in a cookbook or magazine or stashed in your Someday File. Because someday is here. In fact, someday is right now.

THE RECIPES

Quick-ish
Coq au Vin
172

Sticky Pomegranate
Chicken Pieces
174

Wonton Ravioli
with Ricotta and
Spinach
176

Vegetable
Tempura Bowl
178

Stromboli
180

Grilled Thai
Steak Salad
182

Braised Adobo Pork
with Polenta
184

Soba Noodles
with Greens and
Crispy Tofu
186

Grilled Fish
Tacos with
Cilantro Pesto
188

Shrimp and Grits
with Sugar Snaps
and Tomatoes
190

Buttermilk-Herb-
Baked Chicken
Fingers
192

Asian-style
Barbecue Chicken
194

Taco Pizza
196

Sweet and
Spicy Tofu Bowl
198

QUICK-ISH
COQ AU VIN

Is this as luscious as Julia Child's?
No. Does the shortcut version we first whipped
up on that night just after Phoebe
was born make it any less special?
Absolutely not.

Time: 1 hour 15 minutes

1 piece good-quality smoky bacon

¾ cup all-purpose flour

1 tablespoon mustard powder

½ teaspoon smoked paprika

salt and pepper to taste

1 tablespoon olive oil

1¾ pounds bone-in chicken thighs, seasoned with salt and pepper

1 onion, chunked

2 garlic cloves, smushed, but still whole

1 tablespoon tomato paste

1 cup chicken broth

¾ cup red or white wine

1 cup sliced carrots (or more if your kids love these as much as mine do)

1 bunch of thyme, tied with string

handful of white mushrooms, stemmed and sliced

▶ In a Dutch oven or large enamel pot, fry the bacon over medium heat. Remove the bacon when crispy and chop it into smallish pieces. Wipe off a little of the bacon fat in the Dutch oven and raise the heat to medium-high.

▶ Add the flour, mustard powder, paprika, and salt and pepper to a large dinner plate and mix up with your fingers or a fork.

▶ Add the olive oil to the bacon fat in the Dutch oven. Dredge the chicken pieces in the flour mixture, then add to the pot and brown, in batches if necessary, 3 to 4 minutes per side. (They do not have to be cooked through.) Remove to a plate and set aside.

▶ Reduce the heat to medium. Add the onions and garlic to the pot and season with a little more salt and pepper. Stir until the onions are slightly wilted, about 3 minutes. Stir in the tomato paste, then add the chicken broth and wine and whisk until integrated.

▶ Return the chicken to the pot along with the bacon, carrots, thyme, and mushrooms. The chicken should be mostly immersed—add more broth or water if it's not. Bring to a boil, then reduce the heat and simmer for 30 minutes, or until the liquid cooks down a bit. Remove the thyme and the garlic cloves and serve.

Suggested sides: Julia recommends buttered peas and parsley potatoes, so feel free to follow her lead; or try Asparagus with Vinaigrette (page 160) and a baguette.

STICKY POMEGRANATE CHICKEN PIECES

I usually stay away from chicken as a main dish when entertaining (not because I don't like it, but because I just feel like people eat chicken all the time and could use a break), but this is one of the few gloriously delicious exceptions. My kids go crazy for it.

**Time: 1 hour 40 minutes
(mostly hands-off time)**

2 pounds chicken pieces
(we do thighs and
drumsticks)

1 cup low-sodium soy
sauce or tamari

½ cup pomegranate
juice

½ cup sugar

▸ Put a rack in the middle of the oven and preheat the oven to 400°F.

▸ Arrange the chicken in one layer in a foil-lined* roasting pan. Combine the soy sauce, pomegranate juice, and sugar in a small saucepan and cook over low heat, stirring, until the sugar is dissolved. Pour evenly over the chicken pieces. Bake uncovered for 45 minutes. Turn the chicken over and bake until the sauce is thick and sticky, about 45 minutes to an hour more. The sauce should be dark and gooey, but keep an eye on it, so it doesn't get more charred than you like.

*Suggested sides: Dilly Cucumber Salad (page 161);
Rice with Cilantro and Lime (page 162)*

*This is very important! Otherwise you will be left with a massive cleanup job.

WONTON RAVIOLI
with **RICOTTA** *and* **SPINACH**

Homemade ravioli is more art project than dinner project when kids are involved. This recipe calls for about a two-to-one ratio of spinach to ricotta cheese, so if you feel like that's going to be an issue, up the ricotta, decrease the spinach, then gradually sneak more spinach in as they get used to it.

Time: 45 minutes

2 tablespoons olive oil, plus more for drizzling

1 garlic clove, halved

3 tablespoons minced onion

1 cup thawed and well-squeezed frozen spinach

2 tablespoons freshly grated Parmesan, plus more for garnish

½ cup fresh ricotta cheese

grated zest of ½ lemon (about ½ teaspoon)

salt and pepper to taste

40 wonton wrappers, sold at Asian markets (square or round, whatever suits you)

2 cups Homemade Marinara Sauce (page 64) or store-bought tomato sauce

▸ In a skillet set over medium-low heat, heat the oil, then add the garlic, cut side down, and swirl around for a minute so it infuses the oil. Remove the garlic and discard. Add the onions and cook for about a minute, until slightly wilted. Mix in the spinach and stir until it is warmed through. Transfer to a bowl and stir in the Parmesan, ricotta, lemon zest, and salt and pepper.

▸ Lay a few wonton wrappers on a cutting board (keep the remaining wrappers covered with plastic wrap so they don't dry out). Dip your fingers in a bowl of water and "paint" around the edges of the first wrapper. Add about 2 teaspoons of spinach-ricotta filling, cover with another wrapper, smushing the filling gently to flatten, and seal the edges with your fingers. Transfer to a plate. Repeat until all of the wontons are stuffed.

▸ Bring a large pot of water to a boil. In a small saucepan, heat the marinara sauce over medium-low heat.

▸ When the water comes to a boil, gently add the ravioli and cook for 3 minutes, or until they are floating. Drain the ravioli (again, gently) into a colander and drizzle with a little olive oil to prevent sticking.

▸ Serve with the marinara sauce and more Parmesan.

Suggested side: Roasted Cauliflower and Broccoli (page 161)

Note: Some wonton wrappers can be very delicate and sticky. Use a large pot to boil them to prevent clumping, or boil them in two separate pots. These are also great sauceless, topped with chopped fresh basil and Parmesan.

VEGETABLE
TEMPURA BOWL

I can't even tell you how clutch it was to get the kids to like Japanese food. Though they didn't embrace the idea of raw fish immediately, they were huge fans of the sizzling chicken teriyaki platter (shocker) and anything crusted in light tempura batter—from shrimp to broccoli. Turns out, that crust is very easy to re-create at home.

Time: 30 minutes

1 cup uncooked
sushi rice
(enough to yield
3 cups cooked)

1 cup all-purpose flour

1 teaspoon salt

1 cup club soda

$\frac{1}{3}$ cup vegetable or
canola oil, or more
if needed

vegetables such as
asparagus, steamed
broccoli, steamed carrot
coins, steamed onions,
zucchini coins, zucchini
blossoms (don't laugh,
your kids might love it!)

$\frac{1}{4}$ cup seasoned rice
wine vinegar

low-sodium soy sauce,
for dipping

chopped scallions

▸ Prepare the sushi rice according to the package directions.

▸ Meanwhile, make the tempura: In a medium bowl, whisk together the flour and the salt. Pour in the club soda, whisking until it's as smooth as possible. (There will still be little lumps, but that's fine.)

▸ Set a deep-sided skillet or a small Dutch oven over medium-high heat and add the vegetable oil. (The oil should be about $\frac{1}{4}$ inch deep, and is hot enough when a drop of batter sizzles in it.) Dunk the vegetables in the batter so they are coated and let any excess drip off. Add the vegetables to the pan in batches and fry until crispy on both sides, about 3 minutes total. Using a slotted spoon, place them on a paper-towel-lined plate.

▸ When the rice is cooked, toss it with the vinegar. Serve the rice topped with vegetable tempura and offer a bowl of soy sauce mixed with a few scallions for dipping or drizzling.

STROMBOLI

This is one of our go-to dinners for the Super Bowl or the World Series or the American Idol finale or any major televised event that requires our presence on the couch at dinnertime. It can be as big or as small a project as you'd like, depending on how much time you have to make the sauce and dough from scratch. If you go with store-bought, though, it's still every bit as fun for kids.

Time: 1 hour 15 minutes

olive oil for rubbing, plus more for brushing

1 16-ounce store-bought pizza dough,* preferably close to room temperature

¾ cup Homemade Marinara Sauce (page 64) or store-bought pizza sauce (unheated)

8 to 10 fresh basil leaves, chopped

1 tablespoon dried oregano

4 ounces pepperoni or dried sausage, sliced (optional)

handful of red onion slices

roasted red peppers, from a jar (optional)

¾ cup thawed and well-squeezed frozen spinach

8 ounces fresh mozzarella, shredded

8 to 10 dollops fresh ricotta cheese

Freshly grated Parmesan to taste

1 or 2 shakes of red pepper flakes, depending on heat tolerance in your house

Sea salt to taste

▸ Preheat the oven to 350°F.

▸ Rub an 11-by-13-inch cookie sheet bed with olive oil. Using lightly oiled hands, spread the dough on the sheet, pressing it as far into the corners as possible.

▸ Spoon the sauce evenly over the dough, leaving about a 1-inch border. Sprinkle the fresh basil and dried oregano over the sauce. Layer on, in the following order, the pepperoni (if using), onion slices, roasted red peppers (if using), spinach, mozzarella, ricotta, Parmesan, and red pepper flakes.

▸ Very carefully (so as not to tear the dough), starting with a long side, roll the dough and filling into a long cylinder, making sure all the filling is enclosed. You might need two sets of hands to keep it under control. (If the dough does tear, just try to pinch the hole together and keep rolling.) Pinch the bottom and end seams to secure the filling, and place the stromboli seam side down on the cookie sheet. Brush the top with olive oil and sprinkle with sea salt.

▸ Bake for 45 minutes to 1 hour, or until the stromboli is golden brown, brushing again with oil during the last 5 minutes. Allow to cool, about 10 minutes.

▸ Slice into 1½-inch-thick pieces and serve.

Suggested side: **Confetti Kale with Pecorino** *(page 161)*

* For homemade pizza dough, go to dinneralovestory.com/perfect-pizza-crust

GRILLED THAI STEAK SALAD

This is an awesome dinner to make on a summer weekend, when you have time to marinate the steak all day and maybe even work in a meandering stroll through the farmer's market for your produce.

**Time: 30 minutes, plus
2 hours marinating time**

STEAK

$\frac{1}{3}$ cup low-sodium
soy sauce

1 tablespoon lightly
packed brown sugar

1 tablespoon olive oil

1 teaspoon sesame oil

1 bunch of scallions
(white and light green
parts only), chopped

juice of 1 lime

salt and pepper to taste

1 pound flank steak

SALAD

2 cups fresh tender greens
(such as Bibb lettuce)

2 medium carrots, sliced
or peeled with a vegeta-
ble peeler into strips

handful of fresh snow
peas or sugar snap peas

1 red bell pepper,
cored, seeded,
and sliced into strips

handful of roasted salted
peanuts, chopped

$\frac{1}{2}$ cup chopped fresh
mint leaves

$\frac{1}{2}$ cup chopped fresh
cilantro leaves

PEANUT DRESSING

peanut curry sauce
(see page 97)

$\frac{1}{4}$ cup rice wine vinegar

fresh lime juice to taste

▸ Prepare the steak: In a large ziplock bag, combine the soy sauce, brown sugar, olive oil, sesame oil, half of the scallions, the lime juice, and salt and pepper. Add the steak and place the sealed bag on a plate (to catch any drips) in the fridge. Refrigerate for a minimum of 2 hours and up to 8, flipping once halfway through.

▸ While the steak is marinating, assemble the salad ingredients on a platter (or go wild and mix them together), and in a small bowl whisk together the ingredients for the peanut dressing. The salad ingredients can be covered and refrigerated until you are ready to cook the steak, and the dressing can be stored in a covered bowl or jar in the refrigerator.

▸ When it's time to grill, heat a grill pan or an outdoor grill to medium-high. Remove the steak from the marinade and pat it dry to help it sear. Discard the marinade. Cook the steak for about 4 minutes per side (flank steak is thin so it cooks quickly), remove, and let it sit for 10 minutes before cutting. Slice on the bias.

▸ Arrange the slices of steak over the salad, sprinkle with the remaining scallions, and drizzle with the peanut dressing, unless you think that might cause a riot; in which case, just serve the dressing on the side.

BRAISED ADOBO PORK
with POLENTA

You know that Le Creuset Dutch oven you registered for all those years ago? The one that remains spotlessly clean on a high shelf? First of all, no Dutch oven should ever be spotless. Second of all, get to know the pot. In the winter, few things create the Happy Home Vibe as effortlessly as the smell of something braising all day in a Dutch oven. Here's the world's best way to get you started.

Time: 3 hours

2 to 3 tablespoons olive oil

2½-pound pork loin, seasoned with salt and pepper

1 14-ounce can diced tomatoes, with their juice

1 tablespoon dried oregano

½ teaspoon ground cumin

1 bay leaf

1 chipotle in adobo (not the sauce, just the dripping single pepper; you can freeze the rest)

½ cup cider vinegar (or store-bought vinegar-based barbecue sauce such as Shealy's)

2 garlic cloves, halved

1 medium onion, chopped

salt

1 cup medium or fine cornmeal

1 tablespoon butter

½ cup grated sharp Cheddar cheese

handful of chopped fresh cilantro leaves

▸ Preheat the oven to 350°F.

▸ In a Dutch oven or heavy-bottomed ovenproof pot, heat the olive oil over medium-high heat. Brown the pork on all sides in the hot oil, 4 to 5 minutes per side. Remove the pork and add the tomatoes, oregano, cumin, bay leaf, chipotle, cider vinegar, garlic, onions, and ¼ cup water, whisking to combine. Return the pork to the pot; it should be about two-thirds immersed in liquid. Bring to a boil, cover, and place in the oven for 2½ to 3 hours. (The pork should be practically falling apart when finished.)

▸ While the pork is braising, make the polenta: Bring 4 cups salted water to a boil in a heavy saucepan over high heat. Pour the cornmeal into the pot slowly, whisking as you go. The mixture will thicken after 2 or 3 minutes. Reduce the heat and let the mixture bubble on the stovetop for another 40 minutes, stirring every 10 minutes and adding water if it becomes too thick for your liking. Before serving, remove the polenta from the heat and stir in the butter and Cheddar.

▸ Remove the pork from the pot to a cutting board or platter, shred with two forks, and toss back in the braising liquid. Remove the bay leaf.

▸ Sprinkle the cilantro over the pork and serve with the polenta.

SOBA NOODLES *with* GREENS *and* CRISPY TOFU

Full disclosure: I have yet to convince my kids to like this. Which doesn't surprise me, because I'm sort of new to the tofu game myself. But that does not mean we aren't constantly trying. If what the experts say is true—that it takes about twenty-five exposures to a new food before a kid will try a bite— then we are due for a tofu breakthrough any day now.

Time: 45 minutes

1 8-ounce package soba noodles (available in Asian markets or Asian sections of better supermarkets)

1 large bunch of greens, such as kale or spinach (about 4 cups)

1 tablespoon neutral oil (such as vegetable or grapeseed)

3 tablespoons seasoned rice wine vinegar

1 tablespoon soy sauce

½ teaspoon peeled, grated fresh ginger

¼ teaspoon sesame oil

½ teaspoon Sriracha, plus more for garnish

1 scallion (white and light green part only), chopped

3 tablespoons canola or vegetable oil

¼ cup all-purpose flour

½ teaspoon salt

6 ounces extra-firm tofu, pressed (see box) and cut into about ten ½-inch strips (as pictured)

▶ Bring a large pot of water to a boil and prepare the soba noodles according to the package directions. During the last 2 minutes of cooking, drop in the greens Drain together, and toss with the neutral oil in a large bowl.

▶ While noodles cook, whisk together rice wine vinegar, soy sauce, ginger, sesame oil, Sriracha, and scallions. When the noodles and greens are ready, toss them with the soy-ginger dressing in the large bowl.

▶ Heat the canola oil in a medium skillet set over medium-high heat. Mix together flour and salt on a small plate. Dredge each tofu strip in flour, then add to the skillet, shaking first to remove any excess flour. Fry the tofu on both sides until golden and crispy, about 4 minutes total.

▶ Serve the noodles in bowls, topped with two or three tofu strips. Drizzle with Sriracha if desired.

HOW TO PRESS TOFU

Tofu can be watery, which makes it hard to crisp up when cooked. (And makes it way too easy for my eleven-year-old to reject it on the grounds that it tastes like a "flavorless, wet marshmallow.") To solve this, slice your block of tofu lengthwise, place on a plate, cover with a few paper towels, then place a heavy pan on top for at least thirty minutes.

GRILLED FISH TACOS *with* CILANTRO PESTO

I love these because they are crazy delicious, but also because tacos in general provide a good delivery system for debuting new things to the kids. Especially if the new thing happens to be fish.

Time: 35 minutes

FISH

1 tablespoon olive oil

salt and pepper to taste

1-pound mahi-mahi fillet
(or other firm white fish)

juice of ½ lime

8 corn tortillas

CILANTRO PESTO

1 cup cilantro (with stems)

½ cup olive oil

¼ cup pepitas

juice of ½ lime

salt and pepper to taste

dash of hot sauce

TOPPINGS

¼ head of cabbage
(napa or red), chopped
into shreds

1½ cups grape tomatoes
(or any kind of tomatoes,
really), chopped and
tossed with salt and a
drizzle of red wine
vinegar

1 avocado, pitted, peeled,
and chopped

▸ Preheat a grill or grill pan.

▸ Prepare the fish: In a large ziplock bag, combine the olive oil and salt and pepper. Place the fish in the bag, set the bag on a plate (to catch any drips), and let marinate for at least 15 and no longer than 30 minutes at room temperature. Five minutes before you grill, add the lime juice to the marinade.

▸ While the grill heats and the fish marinates, prepare the cilantro pesto: In a mini food processor or blender, combine the cilantro, olive oil, pepitas, lime juice, salt and pepper, and hot sauce. Process until the sauce is the consistency of pesto, scraping down the sides once or twice. Set aside.

▸ Prepare the toppings and set aside.

▸ Once the grill is hot, remove the fillet from the marinade and pat it dry to help it sear. Discard the marinade. Cook the fish for 4 to 5 minutes per side, depending on its thickness. (When it's done, the fish should be firm to the touch but not rock hard. It will flake slightly when pierced with a sharp knife.) Remove the fish from the grill and break it apart into chunks.

▸ Meanwhile, place as many tortillas as can fit on the grill. Flip after 30 seconds, grill a little longer, then transfer to a platter.

▸ Assemble the tacos with the fish and the toppings each family member likes, and drizzle with the pesto.

SHRIMP *and* GRITS *with* SUGAR SNAPS *and* TOMATOES

*This is a classic "When in Rome" dinner in our house:
We make it only when we go on our annual pilgrimage to the beach in South
Carolina. I find travel is always an excellent excuse to convince
the kids to try dishes they wouldn't try at home—and a version of this,
made with fresh Gulf shrimp, was the one that reeled in the girls.*

Time: 40 minutes

1 cup stone-ground white grits

2 tablespoons unsalted butter, plus more if needed

salt and pepper to taste

½ small shallot, chopped

kernels from 1 ear of corn

1 tablespoon vegetable oil

shake of red pepper flakes (optional)

1 cup cherry tomatoes, halved

¼ cup chopped red pepper

1 cup sugar snap peas, trimmed

¾ pound shrimp, peeled and deveined

▸ In a large pot, bring 3 cups salted water to a boil. Stir in the grits, lower the temperature to a simmer, cover, and cook for 20 minutes. When the grits are ready (think cream of wheat consistency), stir in 1 tablespoon of the butter and salt to taste.

▸ While the grits are cooking, in a large skillet over medium heat sauté the shallots and corn with the remaining tablespoon of butter and the vegetable oil. Add the red pepper flakes if your kids can handle it. Cook until the corn looks crispy and brown, about 2 minutes. Push to the sides of the skillet and add the cherry tomatoes, red pepper, and sugar snap peas. After about 2 minutes, push the tomatoes, red bell pepper, and snaps to the sides; add a bit more butter if the skillet is dry, raise the heat a bit, and add the shrimp. Cook for about 1 minute per side. Once the shrimp is cooked, stir in the vegetables.

▸ Spoon the hot grits into 4 bowls. Add the shrimp and vegetable mixture on top.

BUTTERMILK-HERB-BAKED CHICKEN FINGERS

This is for the parents who at some point have said to their children at a higher-than-normal decibel level, "Man cannot survive on chicken fingers alone." Are these chicken fingers? Yes. But are they the greasy, soulless, chickenless kind? Definitely not. The herby marinade makes them just flavorful enough for grown-ups to enjoy, but not so overwhelming that the kids appear mortally wounded at their presence.

Time: 35 minutes plus 1 to 8 hours marinating time

2 cups buttermilk, shaken

½ cup chopped fresh dill

¼ cup chopped fresh chives

leaves from 3 to 4 fresh thyme sprigs

1 garlic clove, halved

3 tablespoons Dijon mustard

4 boneless skinless chicken breasts, pounded flat to even thickness and cut into chicken-finger-size strips

2 cups panko bread crumbs or Kellogg's Corn Flake Crumbs

salt and pepper to taste

▶ In a large bowl, whisk together the buttermilk, dill, chives, thyme, garlic, and mustard. Add the chicken pieces and marinate, covered, in the refrigerator for at least 1 hour and up to 8.

▶ Preheat the oven to 400°F. Coat a rimmed baking sheet lightly with cooking spray.

▶ Pour the panko crumbs onto a large plate and mix in salt and pepper. One by one, remove each chicken finger from the marinade, allowing excess marinade to drip off, and dredge in the crumbs. Place the coated chicken fingers on the baking sheet without crowding. Bake for about 15 minutes, or until firm to the touch, but not rock hard.

Suggested sides: Corn with Butter and Cotija Cheese (page 157); Beets with Feta and Chives (see page 160); Tomatoes with Feta and Balsamic (page 157)

Note: If your kids are dip crazy, try these with honey-mustard on the side. Mix 1 tablespoon honey with 4 tablespoons brown mustard.

ASIAN-STYLE BARBECUE CHICKEN

When you're about to grill chicken and you think to yourself, I wish there were a more exciting way to grill chicken . . . well, here's the solution. Note that this chicken can be cooked in a grill pan, but it will not be as tasty as real–deal grilling over coals.

Time: 30 minutes

6 tablespoons
hoisin sauce

$\frac{1}{8}$ teaspoon Chinese
five-spice powder

1 teaspoon sesame oil

1 garlic clove, halved

$\frac{1}{2}$ medium onion,
chopped into large
chunks

2 tablespoons rice
wine vinegar

1 tablespoon Asian
fish sauce

1 tablespoon low-sodium
soy sauce

1 tablespoon honey

hot pepper paste
or a squeeze of Sriracha
(about $\frac{1}{4}$ teaspoon)

1$\frac{1}{2}$ pounds boneless
chicken thighs

Salt and pepper to taste

4 to 5 lime wedges

▸ In a small saucepan over low heat, whisk together hoisin, five-spice powder, sesame oil, garlic, onions, vinegar, fish sauce, soy sauce, honey, and hot pepper paste. Heat until everything has dissolved, about 10 minutes. Remove the sauce from the stovetop and let cool. Once it's cool, pour into a small bowl. (Any extra sauce keeps for up to a week in the refrigerator.)

▸ Prepare a charcoal grill. Drizzle the chicken pieces with a little oil (canola, vegetable, or grapeseed), salt, and pepper. When the grill is hot, grill the chicken (still sauceless) for 8 to 10 minutes, turning all the while. Brush the chicken with the barbecue sauce and cook another 3 minutes, basting with the sauce the entire time, and turning the pieces frequently so they don't burn. Serve with lime wedges.

Suggested sides: Rice with Cilantro and Lime (page 162); Confetti Kale with Pecorino (page 161)

TACO PIZZA

I know it sounds like something you'd find on the menu at Chuck E. Cheese and not in a book where you'd like to be reminded that you are a grown-up with grown-up gastronomic principles—but the addition of queso fresco, radishes, and fresh lettuce makes this dinner just as rockin' for the big kids as it is for the little ones.

Time: 45 minutes

2 tablespoons olive oil

½ small onion, chopped

2 garlic cloves, minced

¾ pound ground beef, turkey, or chicken*

salt and pepper to taste

2 teapoons dried oregano

1 tablespoon chili powder

pinch of cayenne pepper

1 16-ounce ball whole wheat pizza dough† or store-bought pizza dough

1½ cups sharp Cheddar cheese, shredded

GARNISHES

1½ cups shredded Bibb lettuce

1 to 2 small radishes, sliced into coins

2 to 3 ounces queso fresco, crumbled

½ cup chopped fresh cilantro

1 tablespoon minced red onion

salsa to taste

handful fresh tomatoes, chopped

▶ Preheat the oven to 450°F.

▶ In a medium skillet over medium-low heat, warm the olive oil. Add the onions and garlic and sauté for about 3 minutes. Raise the heat to medium-high, add the meat, breaking up with a fork, and cook, stirring occasionally, until it just loses its pink color, about 5 minutes. Add salt and pepper, the oregano, the chili powder, and the cayenne—get it sizzly so the spices get fragrant. Cook for another 5 minutes.

▶ Meanwhile, using your fingers, press out the pizza dough on a lightly greased rimmed 9-by-13-inch baking sheet until it reaches all four corners. (The dough should be thin.) Leaving a 1-inch border around the perimeter, spoon the seasoned meat evenly across the dough. Sprinkle the Cheddar on top and bake until the cheese is golden and bubbly and the crust is golden, about 15 minutes. Watch carefully so crust doesn't burn.

▶ Remove the baking sheet from the oven and set on a wire rack. Top the pizza with the garnishes, cut into squares, and serve.

* This is also delicious when you replace the ground meat with leftover braised pork (page 184).

† For homemade pizza dough, go to dinneralovestory.com/perfect-pizza-crust

SWEET *and* SPICY TOFU BOWL

Every time I make this, Andy unleashes the magic phrase: "I could eat like this every night." It's light, healthy, and totally open to interpretation. We serve it with spinach, but you can use virtually any vegetable that's fresh at the market; steamed sugar snap peas work well, as do carrots, shallots, cabbage, green beans, asparagus, or zucchini.

Time: 45 minutes

1 14-ounce block
extra-firm tofu

½ cup sweet white miso,
such as Miso Master
brand (available in
Asian markets and in the
refrigerated sections
of better supermarkets)

⅓ cup pure maple syrup

1 tablespoon Sriracha,
plus more for serving

1 tablespoon low-sodium
soy sauce

juice of ½ small lime

2 cups cooked sushi rice,
drizzled with 1 tablespoon
seasoned rice wine
vinegar while still warm

1 bunch of spinach,
sautéed in olive oil,
salted and peppered

Note that the tofu
needs to be pressed for
at least 30 minutes.

▸ About 30 minutes before you plan to start cooking, slice the tofu into pieces the size of playing cards (about ½ inch thick), lay them flat on a paper-towel-lined dinner plate, cover with more paper towels, then place something heavy on top, such as a cast-iron pan. (See the note on pressing tofu, page 187.)

▸ In a small mixing bowl, whisk together the miso, maple syrup, Sriracha, soy sauce, and lime juice.

▸ Preheat the broiler to high. Line a rimmed baking sheet with foil and coat lightly with cooking spray. Place the tofu pieces on the baking sheet, brush with the miso mixture, and broil for 5 minutes, or until golden but not burned. Flip over and broil for another 5 minutes, watching it carefully.

▸ Serve the tofu over the sushi rice with the spinach and a drizzle of Sriracha, if desired.

WORKBOOK

OPERATION 30 DAYS REPORT CARD

Week of: _____

DAY	MEAL	KID TRIED YES/NO?	KEEPER?	COOK'S GRADE	KID'S GRADE
Sunday					
Monday					
Tuesday					
Wednesday					
Thursday					
Friday					
Saturday					

Prize: _____

You can also download this chart at dinneralovestory.com/30days.

OPERATION 30 DAYS REPORT CARD

Week of:

DAY	MEAL	KID TRIED YES/NO?	KEEPER ?	COOK'S GRADE	KID'S GRADE
Sunday					
Monday					
Tuesday					
Wednesday					
Thursday					
Friday					
Saturday					

Prize:

You can also download this chart at dinneralovestory.com/30days.

OPERATION 30 DAYS REPORT CARD

Week of:

DAY	MEAL	KID TRIED YES/NO?	KEEPER ?	COOK'S GRADE	KID'S GRADE
Sunday					
Monday					
Tuesday					
Wednesday					
Thursday					
Friday					
Saturday					

Prize:

You can also download this chart at dinneralovestory.com/30days.

OPERATION 30 DAYS REPORT CARD

Week of:

DAY	MEAL	KID TRIED YES/NO?	KEEPER ?	COOK'S GRADE	KID'S GRADE
Sunday					
Monday					
Tuesday					
Wednesday					
Thursday					
Friday					
Saturday					

Prize:

You can also download this chart at dinneralovestory.com/30days.

OPERATION 30 DAYS REPORT CARD

Week of:

DAY	MEAL	KID TRIED YES/NO?	KEEPER ?	COOK'S GRADE	KID'S GRADE
Sunday					
Monday					
Tuesday					
Wednesday					
Thursday					
Friday					
Saturday					

Prize:

You can also download this chart at dinneralovestory.com/30days.

OPERATION 30 DAYS REPORT CARD

Week of: ....

DAY	MEAL	KID TRIED YES/NO?	KEEPER ?	COOK'S GRADE	KID'S GRADE
Sunday					
Monday					
Tuesday					
Wednesday					
Thursday					
Friday					
Saturday					

Prize: ....

You can also download this chart at dinneralovestory.com/30days.

ACKNOWLEDGMENTS

*At last, my favorite part of writing:
expressing my gratitude to
everyone whose shoulders I stood
upon to crank out this book:*

I'd like to thank . . .

Jennifer Tung, my editor, for her friendship, for her
experienced hand guiding a many-moving-parts book like this
to publication, and for delivering big on every promise.
Even the pie-in-the-sky ones.

Gina Centrello and Libby McGuire for making
me feel like part of the Ballantine family from the moment
I stepped in the office.

The entire Ballantine team: Nina Shield, Susan Corcoran,
Sharon Propson, Carole Lowenstein, Mark Maguire, Richard Callison,
Evan Camfield, Janet McDonald, Maggie Oberrender, Matt Schwartz.
You guys know how to do it.

Elyse Cheney, my agent, whose loyalty and wise counsel
I am grateful for every day.

Kristina DiMatteo, the colossally talented designer
who made the cover and every page of this book sing.

Andy, Phoebe, and Abby, for being my
guinea pigs, my pillars of patience,
my cheerleaders, and my whole entire universe.
Now finish your milk.

INDEX

Page numbers in **bold** are the location of the recipe.

A

advance prep, 41–42, 45, 50–53, 57–59

the adventure, 10–14

anchovies, 43, 112–13

Angel Hair Pasta with Homemade Marinara Sauce, 37, **64–65**

apples, 47

artichokes, 39, **90–91**

Asian Slaw with Chicken, **150–151**, 31

Asian-Style Barbecue Chicken, **194–95**

asparagus

Asparagus and Goat Cheese Tart, 32, **132–33**

Asparagus with Spicy Mayo and Chives, Roasted Salmon and, 32, **66–67**

Asparagus with Vinaigrette, 83, 123, **160**, 173

avocados

Chicken BLTs, 32, **110–11**

Chorizo Tacos with Slaw and Avocado, 30, **106–7**

Grilled Fish Tacos with Cilantro Pesto, 33, **188–89**

Halved Avocado with Vinaigrette, 75, 99, 141, **156**

Kale Cobb Salad, 33, **138–39**

Tomato and Avocado Salad, 31, 145, **156**

B

bacon

Chicken BLTs, 32, **110–11**

Kale Cobb Salad, 33, **138–39**

Pasta with Peas, Bacon, and Ricotta, **94–95**

baguettes, 163

baked beans, 35, 119, 163

Baked Potato Bar, 32, **92–93**

bananas, 47

barbecue

Asian-Style Barbecue Chicken, **194–95**

Basic Barbecue Roasted Chicken, 35, **72–73**

Homemade Barbecue Sauce, 73, **122–23**

Pulled Barbecue Chicken Sandwiches, 30, **122–23**

barley

advance prep, 52–53

Barley with Herbs and Scallions, 67, 83, 117, 143, **159**

Chicken and Barley Soup, **148–49**

Basic Barbecue Roasted Chicken, 35, **72–73**

basic vinaigrette, **51**

beans

advance prep, 53

baked beans, 35, 119, 163

Black Bean and Goat Cheese Quesadillas, 31, **70–71**

black beans, 163

Chicken Chili, 33, **144–45**

Green Beans with Ginger and Garlic, 89, 105, **159**

Green Beans with Toasted Almonds and Mint, 121

White Beans and Spinach, 117, **156**

beef

Grilled Thai Steak Salad, 31, **182–83**

Korean Short Ribs, 37, **120–21**

Steak Sandwiches with Gruyère, 36, **116–17**

Taco Pizza, 38, **196–97**

beets

Beets with Feta and Chives, 39, 147, **160,** 193

bell peppers

Grilled Thai Steak Salad, 31, **182–83**

leftovers, 47

Stromboli, 39, **180–81**

berries, 47

Black Bean and Goat Cheese Quesadillas, 31, **70–71**

black beans, 163

Braised Adobo Pork with Polenta, 38, **184–85**

breads, 47, 163

broccoli

advance prep, 53

leftovers, 47

Roasted Cauliflower and Broccoli, **161,** 177

broccoli logic, 13

Brussels sprouts, 15, **100–101**

burgers, **88–89**

Buttered Peas with Mint, 34, 85, 109, **159**

Buttermilk-Herb-Baked Chicken Fingers, 30, **192–93**

butternut squash, 32, **78–79**

C

carrots

Curried Carrots, 97, **155**

Grilled Thai Steak Salad, 31, **182–83**

Potato-Carrot Hash, **68–69**

cauliflower

Roasted Cauliflower and Broccoli, **161,** 177

Whole Wheat Spaghetti with Roasted Cauliflower and Bread Crumbs, 31, **112–13**

chicken

advance prep, 52

Asian Slaw with Chicken, 31, **150–51**

Asian-Style Barbecue Chicken, **194–95**

Basic Barbecue Roasted Chicken, 35, **72–73**

broth, 48

Buttermilk-Herb-Baked Chicken Fingers, 30, **192–93**

Chicken and Barley Soup, 36, **148–49**

Chicken BLTs, 32, **110–11**

Chicken Chili, 33, **144–45**

Chicken Parm Meatballs, 36, **134–35**

Chicken Sausages with Kale Slaw, 35, **118–19**

Chicken with Artichokes in Creamy Mustard Sauce, 39, **90–91**

Creamy Greek Chicken Noodle Soup, 37, **102–3**

Greens with Chicken, Cherries, Blue Cheese, and Candied Walnuts, 38, **142–43**

Grilled Chicken with Peanut Curry Sauce, **96–97**

Kale Cobb Salad, 33, **138–39**

Pan-Roasted Chicken Thighs with Potato-Carrot Hash, **68–69**

Pulled Barbecue Chicken Sandwiches, 30, **122–23**

Quick-ish Coq au Vin, **172–73**

Sticky Pomegranate Chicken Pieces, 37, **174–75**

Summer Stew with Chicken, Corn, and Sausage, 34, **124–25**

Taco Pizza, 38, **196–97**

chile paste, 43

chili, 33, **144–45**

chipotle chiles in adobo sauce, 43, 123

Braised Adobo Pork with Polenta, 38, **184–85**

Pulled Chicken Barbecue Sandwiches, **122–23**

choosing recipes

Go-To Weeknight Meals, 23–27, 56–63

Keep-the-Spark-Alive Dinners, 23, 24, 26–27, 166–71

meal plans, 27–39

chorizo

Chorizo and Kale Frittata, 34, **82–83**

Chorizo Tacos with Slaw and Avocado, 30, **106–7**

Summer Stew with Chicken, Corn, and Sausage, 34, **124–25**

cider vinegar, 43

cilantro pesto, 33, **189**

Cioppino, 38, **128–29**

Classic School Night meals, 39

commitment, 22, 50

Confetti Kale with Pecorino, 39, 89, 145, **161**, 195

cooking skills, 8–10

Coq au Vin, **172–73**

corn

Corn with Butter and Cotija Cheese, 75, 111, 147, **157**, 193

Shrimp and Grits with Sugar Snaps and Tomatoes, **190–91**

Summer Stew with Chicken, Corn, and Sausage, 34, **124–25**

Cornmeal-Crusted Fish with Homemade Tartar Sauce, 34, **108–9**

Crazy Simple meals, 29

Creamy Greek Chicken Noodle Soup, 37, **102–3**

Creamy Mustard Sauce, 39, **91**

Crispy Rice Omelet, 33, **140–41**

Crock Pot meals, 120–21

cucumbers

Cucumber-Tomato-Parsley Salad, 32, 69, **160**

Dilly Cucumber Salad, 37, 97, **161**, 175

Curried Carrots, 97, **155**

D

Deconstructing Dinner, 13, 15–16

Dilly Cucumber Salad, 37, 97, **161**, 175

Dinner Diary, xii

Dinner: A Love Story (blog), x–xi

Dinner: A Love Story (book), xvii

do-ahead tasks, 41–42, 45, 50–53, 57–59

See also planning

dressings and marinades

basic vinaigrette, **51**

buttermilk-herb marinade, 30, **193**

Peanut Dressing, **183**

See also salads; sauces and salsas

E

Easy Homemade Macaroni and Cheese, 38, **126–27**

eggs

Asparagus and Goat Cheese Tart, 32, **132–33**

Chorizo and Kale Frittata, 34, **82–83**

Crispy Rice Omelet, 33, **140–41**

egg salad sandwich, 47

Kale Cobb Salad, 33, **138–39**

leftovers, 47

Spinach and Feta Omelet, 35, **114–15**

Vegetable-Loaded Fried Rice, 30, **76–77**

Zucchini Fritters with Sour Cream and Chives, 34, **130–31**

F

familiar ingredients, 15–16, 18

family dinner, x–xi, xiii–xvi, 9

Lowest Common Denominator Meals, xv

meal plans, 27–39

nights off, 25

Operation 30 Days, 30 Dinners, xvi–xix, 2–3

rules, 7–19

Team Family Dinner, 49

Family Fave meals, 38

family involvement, 8–14

farmers' markets, 40, 170

fennel seeds, 43

fish, 29

Cioppino, 38, **128–29**

Cornmeal-Crusted Fish with Homemade Tartar Sauce, 34, **108–9**

Grilled Fish Tacos with Cilantro Pesto, 33, **188–89**

Miso-Glazed Salmon, 35, **104–5**

Roasted Salmon and Asparagus with Spicy Mayo and Chives, 32, **66–67**

Roasted Salmon with Lentils, 37, **136–37**

Tomato Fish Stew, 38, **128–29**

See also seafood

fish sauce, 43

flavor-blaster ingredients, 43

flexitarian meals, 9, 32

formula for meal plans, 28–29

freeze ahead instructions, 10

Freezer meals, 29

Friday night out, xviii

frittatas, 34, **82–83**

fruit leftovers, 47

G

getting started. *See* planning

Go-To Weeknight Meals, 23–27, 56–63

grading, 2–3, 18, 44, 202–9

Grains with Vegetables, 73, **158**

green beans

advance prep, 53

Green Beans with Ginger and Garlic, 89, 105, **159**

Green Beans with Toasted Almonds and Mint, 121, **155**

greens

advance prep, 53

Greens with Chicken, Cherries, Blue Cheese, and Candied Walnuts, 38, **142–43**

Grilled Thai Steak Salad, 31, **182–83**

Soba Noodles with Greens and Crispy Tofu, 30, **186–87**

See also salads

Grilled Chicken with Peanut Curry Sauce, **96–97**

Grilled Fish Tacos with Cilantro Pesto, 33, **188–89**

Grilled Thai Steak Salad, 31, **182–83**

grits, **190–91**

H

Halved Avocado with Vinaigrette, 75, 99, 141, **156**

ham, 31, **86–87**

herbs, 48, 53

hoisin sauce, 43

Hoisin Turkey Burgers, **88–89**

Homemade Barbecue Sauce, 73, **122–23**

Homemade Marinara Sauce, 37, **64–65,** 85, 135, 177

Homemade Tartar Sauce, 34, **109**

honey-mustard dip, 193

hot sauce, 43

I

"I Don't Know Yet" decoy, 16–18

ingredients

cheater specials, 163

exploring, 170

familiarity, 15–16, 18

flavor-blasters, 43

freshness, 25–26

security blankets, 26

K

kale

Chicken Sausages with Kale Slaw, 35, 118–19

Chorizo and Kale Frittata, 82–83

Confetti Kale with Pecorino, 39, 89, 145, **161**, 195

Kale Cobb Salad, 33, **138–39**

Keep-the-Spark-Alive Dinners, 23, 24, 26–27, 166–71

kids, 8–14

"I Don't Know Yet" decoy, 16–18

picky eating, xiv–xv, xviii–xix

"try new things" mindset, xvii

Kitchen Dump, 41, 46–48

L

leeks, 31, **86–87**

lentils, 37, **136–37**

Lowest Common Denominator Meals, xv

M

Macaroni and Cheese, 38, **126–27**

make-ahead food, 41–42, 45, 50–53, 57–59

See also planning

Making Dinner Happen, 10

Maple Candy Pork Chops, 39, **146–47**

marinara sauce, 37, **64–65,** 85, 135, 177

meal plans, 27–39

Classic School Night meals, 39

Crazy Simple meals, 29

Family Fave meals, 38

Fish meals, 29

Flexitarian meals, 32

formula for, 28–29

Freezer meals, 29

Meatless meals, 29

Modern Comfort Food meals, 37

My Idea of a Perfect Week meals, 31

Quick and Strategic meals, 33

meal plans (*cont'd*):

Summer Fresh meals, 34

Super-Fast meals, 35

Super Simple meals, 30

Use-It-or-Lose-It meals, 29

Winter Warm-Your-Bones meals, 36

meatballs, 36, **134–35**

Meatless meals, 29

miso, 43

Miso-Glazed Salmon, 35, **104–5**

Modern Comfort Food meals, 37

mustard sauce, 39, **91**

My Idea of a Perfect Week meals, 31

N

naming recipes, 13

nights off, 25

noodles. *See* pasta and noodles

notes, 202–9

after-the-meal notes, 18, 44

make-ahead notes, 41–42

report cards, 2–3, 18, 44

O

omelets

Crispy Rice Omelet, 33, **140–41**

Spinach and Feta Omelet, 35, **114–15**

Operation 30 Days, 30 Dinners, xvi–xix, 2–3

P

pancakes, 47

Pan-Fried Whole Wheat Pizzas, 36, **84–85**

Pan-Fried Whole Wheat Pizzas with Ham and Leeks, **86–87**

Pan-Roasted Chicken Thighs with Potato-Carrot Hash, **68–69**

pasta and noodles

Angel Hair Pasta with Homemade Marinara Sauce, 37, **64–65**

Easy Homemade Macaroni and Cheese, 38, **126–27**

Pasta with Peas, Bacon, and Ricotta, **94–95**

Pasta with Roasted Butternut Squash and Paprika, 32, **78–79**

Penne with Roasted Tomatoes and Spinach, 35, **80–81**

Soba Noodles with Greens and Crispy Tofu, 30, **186–87**

Spaghetti with Shallots and Brussels Sprouts, **100–101**

Whole Wheat Spaghetti with Roasted Cauliflower and Bread Crumbs, 31, **112–13**

Wonton Ravioli with Ricotta and Spinach, **176–77**

Peanut Curry Sauce, **97**

Peanut Dressing, **183**

peas

Buttered Peas with Mint, 34, 85, 109, **159**

Pasta with Peas, Bacon, and Ricotta, **94–95**

Shrimp and Grits with Sugar Snaps and Tomatoes, **190–91**

Sugar Snap Pea and Radish Salad, 35, 105, 121, **157**

Penne with Roasted Tomatoes and Spinach, 35

pesto, 33, **189**

picky eating, xiv–xv, xviii–xix, 12–13

Deconstructing Dinner, 13, 15–16

getting involved, 8–14

shopping, 14

pizzas

Pan-Fried Whole Wheat Pizzas, 36, **84–85**

Pan-Fried Whole Wheat Pizzas with Ham and Leeks, 31, **86–87**

Taco Pizza, 38, **196–97**

planning, xi, 22–53, 56–59

advance prep, 41–42, 45, 50–53, 57–59

commitment, 22, 50

family involvement, 8–14, 22

family rules, 7–19

gathering recipes, 23–27

meal plans, 27–39

shopping, 14, 40–41

point and cook, 13

polenta, 38, **184–85**

pork

Braised Adobo Pork with Polenta, 38, **184–85**

Slow-Cooker Korean Short Ribs, 37, **120–21**

Maple Candy Pork Chops, 39, **146–47**

potatoes

Baked Potato Bar, 32, **92–93**

Chorizo and Kale Frittata, 34, **82–83**

Potato-Carrot Hash, **68–69**

prepared horseradish, 43

pressed tofu, 187

psychological latch food, 15–16

Pulled Barbecue Chicken Sandwiches, 30, **122–23**

Q

quesadillas, 31, **70–71**

Quick and Strategic meals, 33

Quick Creamed Spinach, 87, 109, **158**

Quick-ish Coq au Vin, **172–73**

quinoa, 52–53

R

ravioli, **176–77**

report cards, 2–3, 18, 44, 202–9

restaurant favorites, 13

rewards, 18

rice

Crispy Rice Omelet, 33, **140–41**

Rice with Cilantro and Lime, 37, 71, **162**, 175, 195

Sweet and Spicy Tofu Bowl, 33, **198–99**

Vegetable-Loaded Fried Rice, 30, **76–77**

Vegetable Tempura Bowl, 39, **178–79**

rice wine vinegar, 43

Roasted Beets with Feta and Chives, 39, 147, **160**, 193

Roasted Cauliflower and Broccoli, **161**, 177

Roasted Salmon and Asparagus with Spicy Mayo and Chives, 32, **66–67**

Roasted Salmon with Lentils, 37, **136–37**

roasted tomatoes, 47–48

rules, 7–19

familiar ingredients, 15–16, 18

family involvement, 8–14, 22, 49

fun, 10–14

getting started, 7–8

"I Don't Know Yet" decoy, 16–18

keeping notes, 18

report cards, 18

rewards, 18

weekly shopping, 14

S

salads, **156–63**

Asian Slaw with Chicken, 31, **150–51**

Asparagus with Vinaigrette, 83, 123, **160**, 173

Beets with Feta and Chives, 39, 147, **160**, 193

Confetti Kale with Pecorino, 39, 89, 145, **161**, 195

Cucumber-Tomato-Parsley Salad, 32, 69, **160**

Dilly Cucumber Salad, 37, 97, **161**, 175

Greens with Chicken, Cherries, Blue Cheese, and Candied Walnuts, 38, **142–43**

Grilled Thai Steak Salad, 31, **182–83**

Halved Avocado with Vinaigrette, 75, 99, 141, **156**

Kale Cobb Salad, 33, **138–39**

Kale Slaw, 35, **118–19**

lentil salad, 137

Sandwich Slaw, 123, **162**

Sugar Snap Pea and Radish Salad, 35, 105, 121, **157**

Tomato and Avocado Salad, 31, 145, **156**

Tomatoes with Feta and Balsamic, 33, 141, **157**, 193

salmon

Miso-Glazed Salmon, 35, **104–5**

Roasted Salmon and Asparagus with Spicy Mayo and Chives, 32, **66–67**

Roasted Salmon with Lentils, 37, **136–37**

sandwiches

Chicken BLTs, 32, **110–11**

egg salad sandwich, 47

Pulled Barbecue Chicken Sandwiches, 30, **122–23**

Shrimp Rolls, 34, **74–75**

Sloppy Joes, 39, **98–99**

Steak Sandwiches with Gruyère, 36, **116–17**

Stromboli, 39, **180–81**

Sandwich Slaw, 123, **162**

sauces and salsas

Cilantro Pesto, 33, **189**

Creamy Mustard Sauce, 39, **91**

flavor blasters, 43

Homemade Barbecue Sauce, 73, **122–23**

sauces and salsas (cont'd):

    Homemade Marinara Sauce, 37, **64–65**, 85, 135, 177

    Homemade Tartar Sauce, 34, **109**

    Peanut Curry Sauce, **97**

    Spicy Mayo and Chives, 32, **66–67**

    See also dressings and marinades

sausage

    Chicken Sausages with Kale Slaw, 35, **118–19**

    Chorizo and Kale Frittata, 34, **82–83**

    Chorizo Tacos with Slaw and Avocado, 30, **106–7**

    Stromboli, 39, **180–81**

    Summer Stew with Chicken, Corn, and Sausage, 34, **124–25**

Sautéed Spinach with Garlic, 36, 85, 87, 113, **155**

seafood

    Cioppino, 38, **128–29**

    Shrimp and Grits with Sugar Snaps and Tomatoes, **190–91**

    Shrimp Rolls, 34, **74–75**

    See also fish

security blanket ingredients, 26

shopping, 14, 40–42

    lists, 27, 40–41

    unpacking and advance prep, 41–42

shrimp

    Cioppino, 38, **128–29**

    Shrimp and Grits with Sugar Snaps and Tomatoes, **190–91**

    Shrimp Rolls, 34, **74–75**

sides, 69, **153–63**

    Barley with Herbs and Scallions, 67, 83, 117, 143, **159**

    Buttered Peas with Mint, 34, 85, 109, **159**

    cheater specials, 163

    Corn with Butter and Cotija Cheese, 75, 111, 147, **157**, 193

    Curried Carrots, 97, **155**

    Green Beans with Ginger and Garlic, 89, 105, **159**

    Green Beans with Toasted Almonds and Mint, 121, **155**

    Quick Creamed Spinach, 87, 109, **158**

    Rice with Cilantro and Lime, 37, 71, **162**, 175, 195

    Roasted Cauliflower and Broccoli, **161**, 177

    Sautéed Spinach with Garlic, 65, 85, 87, 113, 135, **155**

    White Beans and Spinach, 117, **156**

    Whole Grains with Vegetables, 73, **158**

    See also salads

slaw

    Asian Slaw with Chicken, 31, **150–51**

    Kale Slaw, 35, **118–19**

    Sandwich Slaw, 123, **162**

Sloppy Joes, 39, **98–99**

Slow-Cooker Korean Short Ribs, **120–21**

smoked paprika, 43, 78–79

smoothies, 47

Soba Noodles with Greens and Crispy Tofu, 30, **186–87**

soups

    Chicken and Barley Soup, **148–49**

    Cioppino, 38, **128–29**

    Creamy Greek Chicken Noodle Soup, 37, **102–3**

    vegetable broth, 48

spaghetti. See pasta and noodles

Spaghetti with Shallots and Brussels Sprouts, 36, **100–101**

Spark Dinners. See Keep-the-Spark-Alive-Dinners

spinach

    Penne with Roasted Tomatoes and Spinach, 35, **80–81**

    Quick Creamed Spinach, 87, 109, **158**

    Sautéed Spinach with Garlic, 65, 85, 87, 113, 135, **155**

    Spinach and Feta Omelet, 35, **114–15**

    Stromboli, 39, **180–81**

    Sweet and Spicy Tofu Bowl, 33, **198–99**

    White Beans and Spinach, 117, **156**

    Wonton Ravioli with Ricotta and Spinach, **176–77**

squash

    Pasta with Roasted Butternut Squash and Paprika, 32, **78–79**

    Zucchini Fritters with Sour Cream and Chives, 34, **130–31**

Sriracha sauce, 43

starting. See planning

steak

    Grilled Thai Steak Salad, 31, **182–83**

Steak Sandwiches with Gruyère, 36, **116–17**

Sticky Pomegranate Chicken Pieces, 37, **174–75**

Stromboli, 39, **180–81**

Sugar Snap Pea and Radish Salad, 35, 105, 121, **157**

Summer Fresh meals, 34

Summer Stew with Chicken, Corn, and Sausage, 34, **124–25**

Super-Fast meals, 35

Super Simple meals, 30

Sweet and Spicy Tofu Bowl, 33, **198–99**

sweet potato fries, 39, 99, 111, 147, 163

T

tacos
    Chorizo Tacos with Slaw and Avocado, 30, **106–7**

    Grilled Fish Tacos with Cilantro Pesto, 33, **188–89**

    Taco Pizza, 38, **196–97**

tartar sauce, 34, **109**

tarts, 32, **132–33**

Team Family Dinner, 49

tofu
    pressing, 187

    Soba Noodles with Greens and Crispy Tofu, 30, **186–87**

    Sweet and Spicy Tofu Bowl, 33, **198–99**

tomatoes
    Chicken BLTs, 32, **110–11**

    Chicken Chili, 33, **144–45**

    Cioppino, 38, **128–29**

Cucumber-Tomato-Parsley Salad, 32, 69, **160**

Grilled Fish Tacos with Cilantro Pesto, 33, **188–89**

Homemade Marinara Sauce, 37, **64–65**, 85, 135, 177

leftovers, 47–48

Penne with Roasted Tomatoes and Spinach, 35, **80–81**

Shrimp and Grits with Sugar Snaps and Tomatoes, **190–91**

Taco Pizza, 38, **196–97**

Tomato and Avocado Salad, 31, 145, **156**

Tomatoes with Feta and Balsamic, 33, 141, **157**, 193

Tomato Fish Stew, 38, **128–29**

turkey
    Hoisin Turkey Burgers, **88–89**

    Sloppy Joes, 39, **98–99**

    Taco Pizza, 38, **196–97**

U

Use-It-or-Lose-It meals, 29

V

vegan before 6 P.M., 9

Vegetable-Loaded Fried Rice, 30

vegetables
    advance prep, 53

    leftovers, 47–48

Vegetable Tempura Bowl, 39, **178–79**

vinaigrette, **51**

W

weekly tasks
    advance prep, 41–42, 45, 50–53, 57–59

    Kitchen Dump, 41, 46–48

    meal plans, 27–39

    shopping, 14, 27, 40–41, 58

weeknight cooking, 23–26

White Beans and Spinach, 117, **156**

whole grains
    advance prep, 52–53

    Barley with Herbs and Scallions, 67, 83, 117, 143, **159**

    Chicken and Barley Soup, **148–49**

    Whole Grains with Vegetables, 73, **158**

    See also rice

whole wheat flatbread, 163

whole wheat pizzas
    with Ham and Leeks, 31, **86–87**

    with Homemade Marinara Sauce, 36, **84–85**

Whole Wheat Spaghetti with Roasted Cauliflower and Bread Crumbs, 31, **112–13**

Winter Warm-Your-Bones meals, 36

Wonton Ravioli with Ricotta and Spinach, **176–77**

Z

Zucchini Fritters with Sour Cream and Chives, 34, **130–31**

ABOUT THE AUTHOR

Jenny Rosenstrach writes the blog
Dinner: A Love Story. She is the author of *Dinner: A Love
Story* (Ecco, 2012) and, with her husband,
Andy Ward, co-writes "The Providers" column for
Bon Appétit. She lives with Andy and their
two daughters in Westchester County, New York.